About the author

Judy Ridgway is a full-time cookery writer and consultant with over twenty cookery books to her name, covering topics as diverse as vegetarian gourmet cooking, home preserving, barbecues, fish cookery, toasted sandwiches and children's books. She also does some broadcasting and consultancy work and runs a small catering business in the London area called London Cooks.

Cooking with
NUTS &
CEREALS
— Judy Ridgway —

CENTURY PUBLISHING
LONDON

First published in Great Britain in 1985
by Century Publishing Co. Ltd,
Portland House,
12–13 Greek Street, London W1V 5LE

ISBN 0 7126 0782 X

Line drawings by Sue Sharples

Set in Linotron Palatino by
Rowland Phototypesetting Ltd,
Bury St Edmunds, Suffolk

Printed in Great Britain in 1985 by
Hunt Barnard Printing Co. Ltd, Aylesbury, Bucks.

Contents

Note: unless otherwise stated, all quantities given serve four people.

Introduction

With the exception of wheat and rice and perhaps peanuts, nuts and cereals have been largely neglected in twentieth century European cookbooks. Yet half the world lives on millet or on corn as their staple diet. Even committed vegetarians have not explored the full potential of these protein-rich foods and newcomers to vegetarian eating probably don't even know the names of some of them.

It's not that there is limited choice, for the health food shops offer almost every kind of cereal in all kinds of guises ranging from whole grains through flaked and cracked varieties, to ground meal and flour. Nuts, too, come in all shapes and sizes both in their shells and out of them. There are flaked nuts, nibbed nuts, ground nuts and even nut flour and many of these products together with some cereals are available on the general supermarket shelves.

When I first encountered this bewildering array of interesting food I really wasn't sure which to choose and once chosen what to do with it. So I looked to the packs themselves, but unfortunately there is not much information given on the majority of them. I then turned to the bookshelves – and found a distinct lack of information here, too.

The only thing to do was to set to and start testing and experimenting for myself. The results of my efforts have been gathered together here to form this book which I hope will benefit both the initiated and the uninitiated.

Some of the recipes will only be suitable for lacto-vegetarians but quite a number of them have been devised with vegans in mind. In addition, many of the recipes which use milk or soft cheese can be made just as successfully using soya milk or tofu. The result is, if anything, slightly 'creamier'!

Finally I would like to thank Kate Frears who has worked with me on the book and who has tried out many of the recipes. She is not a vegetarian but has become quite a convert to many of the ingredients which she viewed with some suspicion at the start of the testing programme. I would also like to thank Whitworth Foods for providing many of the nuts and some of the cereals used in the recipes.

Judy Ridgway

CHAPTER ONE

Choice and Selection

The choice of nuts and cereals available nowadays is extensive. There are nearly a dozen kinds of nuts on sale in the supermarkets. Add to these nuts like macadamia nuts and gingko nuts which can sometimes be found in Japanese or Chinese grocers and the possible variations on a theme are many. Canned water chestnuts can also be included here for they are related both to chestnuts and surprisingly, to buckwheat.

Some nuts, of course, have a very high calorie-to-protein ratio, usually because of their high fat content, but provided they are not used to excess even these nuts can benefit the vegetarian diet.

Cereals, on the other hand, can only be viewed with unqualified enthusiasm. They provide both protein and almost fat-free energy. They are extremely versatile. They are relatively cheap and they are fun to experiment with.

With both nuts and cereals it is worth remembering that their usable protein content can be increased by eating them with other foods containing complementary proteins. Good combinations are cereals with milk products or with pulses such as dried peas, beans and lentils or peanuts which are actually legumes not nuts. Another useful complementary combination is nuts or seeds and pulses. Because they are actually legumes, peanuts can be useful to include with other nuts in nut roasts and rissoles. The addition of dairy produce can also help to fill in the amino acid gaps.

Nuts

ALMONDS

Almonds are one of the most popular nuts worldwide and they probably appear in a larger variety of dishes than any others. They are grown in the temperate zones of the world.

Almonds may be bought in their shells at Christmas time but they are more usually available shelled. They may be purchased blanched or unblanched, halved, flaked, ground or chopped. The latter are sometimes known as nibbed almonds. Ground almonds mixed with sugar may also be bought as marzipan or almond paste. Some almonds are sold roasted and salted.

Look for all but almonds in their shells in the supermarket shelves and in their shells at the greengrocer.

Nutrition. Almonds have a fairly high protein content and a medium fat content compared with other nuts. They also offer dietary fibre and plenty of calcium, potassium, phosphorous and iron. Vitamins present include the B group and E. Their calorie count is 160 calories per 25 g/1 oz.

Preparation. To blanch almonds which retain their brown skins, place in a pan of cold water and bring to the boil. Remove the nuts at once with a slotted spoon. To remove the skins, nip off one end and squeeze the nut out of its skin between finger and thumb.

To toast whole, flaked or ground almonds, place in the grill pan and set under a hot grill for about 1 minute. Stir with a fork to turn the nuts. Alternatively, brown in a dry non-stick frying pan over a low heat.

To salt almonds, grill lightly all over, then fry in oil until well coated and slightly browned. Sprinkle with salt, cool and store in airtight jars.

Uses. In addition to almond paste and marzipan-based petit fours, ground almonds are used in macaroon and japonaise biscuits and cakes and as a filling in Middle Eastern pastries. They may be used to replace some of the flour in cakes, which will give a moister effect and help the keeping qualities of the cakes. Whole almonds are also used as cake decorations.

In savoury foods almonds may be used in stuffings, sauces and salads. Toasted or fried almonds are used in classic dishes such as Trout with Almonds and Cauliflower Amandine. They can also be used as coatings for fried and baked foods and in stir-fry dishes. Salted almonds are commonly served with drinks.

BRAZIL NUTS
These three-sided nuts have an extremely hard outer shell and, as their name suggests, they come from Brazil.

Brazil nuts may be bought in their shells over the Christmas period. Otherwise they are available shelled and whole or flaked.

Buy shelled Brazil nuts at the supermarkets and unshelled ones at the greengrocers.

Nutrition. Brazil nuts have a higher fat content than almost any other nut. They are also fairly rich in protein and dietary fibre. Minerals present include magnesium, zinc, phosphorous and calcium, and vitamins include the B group and E. Their calorie count is 175 calories per 25 g/1 oz.

Preparation. Shelled Brazil nuts are ready to use. Toast flaked Brazils under the grill or in a dry frying pan. To salt whole Brazils fry in plenty of butter for 3–4 minutes. For different flavours add cayenne, chilli powder or curry powder to the fat.

Transfer to a baking tin, sprinkle with salt and roast at 200°C/ 400°F/Gas 6 for 20–25 minutes.

Uses. Brazil nuts are used mainly in sweetmeats and in the nut bowl. However, they can be used to good advantage in stir-fry dishes and in vegetable salads and fruit dishes. Sprinkle onto the morning cereals or muesli. Try them also in nut-based stuffings and nut loaves. They are often best cooked with other nuts for a blend of flavours.

CASHEW NUTS

Cashew nuts are found hanging at the base of the small pear-shaped fruit of the cashew tree. These nuts have a fairly soft texture and a subtle flavour.

They are usually sold loose and shelled and may be lightly roasted and salted. They are available in supermarkets and in larger packs in health food shops.

Nutrition. The protein content of cashew nuts is as good as almonds but not as high as peanuts and the fat content is fairly low. There are virtually no carbohydrates present. Vitamins and minerals present include B group vitamins, vitamin A, calcium and iron. Their calorie count is 160 calories per 25 g/1 oz.

Preparation. Chop or grind for use in savouries, cakes and biscuits. Toast under the grill or in a dry frying pan as for almonds.

To salt cashew nuts, fry gently in oil until browned all over. Drain on kitchen paper and sprinkle with salt.

Uses. Salted cashews are a popular cocktail snack. They are often used in Chinese cooking in dishes such as Stir-Fried Chicken. Toasted cashews are very good sprinkled on both fruit- and vegetable-based salads and on cooked vegetables.

Ground cashew nuts can be used in stuffings and nut rissoles and in sauces.

CHESTNUTS

Known as Spanish or sweet chestnuts in the UK to distinguish them from the inedible horse chestnuts, these nuts are on sale from greengrocers during the late autumn and winter. Hot roasted chestnuts are sold by street traders during the same period. Fresh chestnuts can be stored in a cool dry place for several weeks.

Canned chestnuts, both whole or puréed and sweetened or unsweetened, can be bought from the supermarket. Some health food stores also sell dried chestnuts.

Nutrition. Unlike many of the other nuts chestnuts are low in proteins and fats and rich in carbohydrates. They also contain less dietary fibre than other nuts. Vitamins and minerals present are potassium, B group vitamins and vitamin E. Their calorie count is a low 48 calories per 25 g/1 oz.

Preparation. Chestnuts have a smooth brown inner skin which must be removed before use. This can be done either by roasting or by boiling. The latter method is used for dessert nuts and the former for savoury dishes or prior to puréeing.

To roast chestnuts, slit the surface on the domed face of the nuts or make crosswise slits on the hollow side. Place in a baking tin with a little hot water and roast at 220°C/425°F/Gas 7 for 10–15 minutes. Peel while they are still hot. Some people roast chestnuts in an open fire, but this can be dangerous for they may explode.

To boil chestnuts slit the surface as above and boil for about 5 minutes. Peel while they are still hot. Simmer in stock and use as indicated in the recipe or purée and use. If serving as a purée mix with butter and dot the top with butter to prevent a crust forming. For sweet applications simmer in water or sugar and water.

Soak dried chestnuts in cold water overnight and then proceed as for fresh skinned nuts. Canned chestnuts are already cooked and ready for use.

Uses. Chestnut purée was traditionally served with roast pork and with duck. Chestnuts also make an excellent stuffing and they can be mixed with other vegetables such as cabbage or used in soups and sauces.

Sweet applications include traditional French desserts such as Chestnut Vacherin and Buche de Noël.

COCONUTS

Coconuts grow in bunches on huge tropical palm trees. Consequently they have quite a journey to get to the UK, and this may mean that their juices have dried up before they reach the shops. Check by shaking; you should be able to hear the juice moving around inside the coconut.

These juices are sometimes known as coconut milk but this is misleading for the coconut milk or cream referred to in Eastern recipes is made by pressing the grated flesh of the nut or by steeping it in hot water.

Coconut is also available from the supermarket either in its dried or desiccated form or as a solid block of creamed coconut.

Nutrition. Compared to most other nuts coconut is extremely fatty and its protein content is fairly low. The dietary fibre content is high and it also has B vitamins and potassium to offer. Its calorie count is 100 calories per 25 g/1 oz for fresh coconut, 172 calories per 25 g/1 oz for desiccated coconut and 218 calories per 25 g/1 oz for creamed coconut.

Preparation. To shell whole coconuts start by piercing the three basal pores of the coconut. These are the small bald patches often known as 'eyes'. These sections are softer than the rest of the shell and can easily be pierced with a skewer. Drain out the juices. The shell can now be broken open by dropping onto a concrete surface or hitting hard with a hammer. The coconut will also crack open if placed in a hot oven for a few minutes. Remove the flesh from the skin and grate or process in a food processor.

To make coconut milk add 150 ml/¼ pint water to the freshly grated coconut and leave to stand for 15–20 minutes. To extract the milk squeeze out into a bowl, and squeeze again. To extract more milk soak the squeezed flesh in a further 150 ml/¼ pint water for 10–15 minutes. Squeeze out again and use this thinner liquid to dilute the first thick milk.

Desiccated coconut can be used to make coconut milk in much the same way, but in this case you will need hot water. Pour about 75–100 ml/3–4 fl oz hot water onto 225 g/8 oz desiccated coconut and leave to stand for 1 hour. Squeeze out very well.

To make coconut milk from a slab of creamed coconut, dilute 50 g/2 oz creamed coconut with 150 ml/¼ pint hot water.

To toast grated or dessicated coconut, spread it out evenly over the bottom of a grill pan and grill under a very low heat. Shake the pan and turn the coconut over during cooking. Watch the coconut all the time as it will burn very easily indeed. Coloured coconut is sometimes used for cake decorations or for sweetmeats. To make this place the dessicated coconut in a small bowl and add a very few drops of food colouring. Stir briskly to get an even colour, and add more colour, a drop at a time, if too pale. Spread the coconut out on a baking tray and dry out in a very cool oven. Shake the tray from time to time and turn the coconut over while it dries.

Uses. In Western cooking coconut is used mainly in cakes, biscuits and sweetmeats. In Eastern cooking the flesh may be used for chutney and in some curries, but more frequently the flesh is used to make coconut milk and this is used to flavour curries, rice dishes and desserts.

Toasted coconut makes an attractive decoration or garnish not only for cakes but also for salads and vegetable dishes.

HAZELNUTS

Generally speaking, filberts are the variety of hazelnut most usually found in the shops at Christmas time, though Kent-grown cob nuts may be available from greengrocers in the late autumn. These are the newly formed nuts and they are best eaten raw.

The older dried nuts may be sold in their shells for use as dessert nuts but more often they are sold shelled or sometimes ground. Roast and salted nuts are also on sale for nibbling with drinks.

Hazelnut flour can be bought in some health food shops. It should be used sparingly for it has a very strong flavour.

Nutrition. Hazelnuts offer a reasonable protein level without too high a fat content which makes them a particularly useful culinary nut. They also contain small amounts of dietary fibre and some B group vitamins. They are particularly rich in vitamin E. Their calorie count is 108 calories per 25 g/1 oz.

Preparation. For some applications such as cakes and nut butter, hazelnuts need to be skinned. To do this place the nuts on a baking tray and bake in a moderate oven until the skins can be removed by rubbing together in a bag. Alternatively toast under a low grill heat, shaking the pan from time to time to turn the nuts over.

To use hazelnuts chop coarsely or grind in a mill. Use whole as a decoration or for salting. Remove the skins and use the same method for salting as for almonds or toss in spiced egg white until well coated and bake on a greased baking tray for 30 minutes at 160°C/325°F/Gas 3. Toast whole, chopped or ground to bring out the flavour for use in salads or dry fry in a non-stick frying pan.

Uses. Hazelnuts are used mainly in cakes, pastries, desserts and sweetmeats. Try adding chopped nuts to apple pie or use in a crumble topping or in muesli. But they can also be used in savoury dishes and they make an excellent base for nut loaves and rissoles. Try them also in salads with cubed cheese and watercress or toasted with grated carrot and in nut breads.

PEANUTS

Strictly speaking these are not nuts at all but legumes. However, they are usually treated as nuts and so they are included here. They grow underground in straw-coloured, wrinkled pods.

They are sometimes sold in these pods but more often they are sold shelled, roasted and salted.

Unsalted peanuts are on sale in some supermarkets and in health food shops where they can also be obtained chopped or ground. Peanuts are made into peanut butter and sold in jars either in smooth or crunchy form. Some of the peanut crop also goes to making peanut or groundnut oil. This is a particularly useful vegetable oil as it has virtually no flavour of its own.

Nutrition. Peanuts are particularly rich in protein, matching Brazil nuts and pine nuts. However, their fat content is also fairly high. Peanuts also offer the B group of vitamins, vitamin E, iron, zinc, potassium and a small amount of dietary fibre. Their calorie content is 162–168 calories to 25 g/1 oz for fresh and salted peanuts and 177 calories to 25 g/1 oz for peanut butter.

Preparation. Remove the skins in just the same way as for hazelnuts, and salt or spice as for almonds or hazelnuts. Toast under the grill or dry-fry in a non-stick frying pan.

Uses. Peanuts are extremely versatile and economical which makes them an attractive buy for vegetarians. Use in soups, sauces, stews and nut loaves or rissoles. Toast and use in salads or with vegetables. Use ground or chopped peanuts in cakes, biscuits and teabreads and toast for decorations or sweetmeats.

PECAN NUTS

These American nuts are similar to walnuts but they have the advantage of being less bitter and slightly milder in flavour when cooked. Also their shells are smoother and thinner and much easier to crack. They are available in their shells for Christmas (check your local greengrocer) or shelled at the supermarket or health food shop.

Nutrition. Pecans are less fatty than walnuts but their fat content is still fairly high. They have a medium protein content and also offer potassium, phosphorous and some of the B vitamins.

Preparation. Pecans do not need to be blanched or skinned and may be used whole, chopped or ground. Salt or spice as for almonds.

Uses. Pecans can be used for much the same recipes as for walnuts. They are a 'must' for the traditional American pecan pie and for pecan ice cream. Try also in salads such as coleslaw or scattered over a tomato and sweetcorn salad.

PINE NUTS

Pine nuts or kernels come from pine trees which are native to the Mediterranean area and they are particularly popular in the cooking of the Eastern Mediterranean region. They are almost always sold shelled and ready to use. These small, creamy torpedo-shaped nuts have a very special flavour. However, they do tend to be rather expensive. They can be bought in some supermarkets and in health food shops.

Nutrition. These nuts contain more fat than any of the others except Brazil nuts. They have a medium protein content and very high levels of potassium, phosphorous and iron and some of the B group of vitamins. Their calorie count is a high 180 calories per 25 g/1 oz.

Preparation. Pine nuts require little or no preparation. They may be used whole or chopped. Toast under the grill or in a dry non-stick frying pan.

Uses. Pine nuts appear in savoury dishes such as Moussaka and Stuffed Vine Leaves. They also form one of the basic ingredients, with basil and garlic, of the Italian pesto sauce for pasta. They add interest to many vegetable dishes and salads. Sweet applications include mixing with honey for Greek pastries and special cakes and biscuits.

PISTACHIO NUTS

These pale green nuts with their very distinctive flavour originate in the Middle East. They are usually sold in their shells but with the shell ready open. Some health food shops stock ready-shelled pistachios. However, these tend to be particularly expensive.

Nutrition. Pistachio nuts compare with almonds and cashews for protein and with almonds in their fat content. They have extremely high levels of vitamin A. Their calorie count is 180 calories per 25 g/1 oz.

Preparation. Nuts in their shells can quite easily be removed by forcing the two halves of the shell apart. The nuts will then need skinning. To do this spread on a baking tray and bake in a moderate oven until the skin comes off when the nuts are rubbed together, or toast gently under the grill and rub the nuts together in a bag.

Uses. These attractive nuts may be used whole for decorative effect in pâtés and terrines or they may be chopped and used to give added flavour to stuffings, nut loaves and rissoles. They are also used in desserts, cakes and sweetmeats.

WALNUTS

These nuts are very popular in the UK, both as a dessert nut and as a flavouring for cakes and puddings. Whole nuts in their shells will be on sale in greengrocers and supermarkets over the Christmas period. Unripe nuts are sometimes sold for pickling.

Shelled nuts, either in complete halves or in broken pieces, are on sale all the year round in most supermarkets.

Walnuts are used to manufacture walnut oil. This is best used as salad oil for it has a distinctly nutty flavour to it.

Walnut flour is available in some health food shops but should be used sparingly as it has a very strong flavour.

Nutrition. Walnuts have a high fat content and a reasonable protein level. They also offer small quantities of dietary fibre and vitamin A, B group and E, together with zinc, iron and phosphorous. Their calorie content is 149 calories per 25 g/1 oz.

Preparation. Once shelled, walnuts need very little preparation. They may be used whole for decoration or chopped or ground in cakes and savoury dishes. Dry-toasting walnuts in a non-stick pan brings out the flavour for sprinkling over salads and they can also be salted in the same way as almonds.

Uses. The traditional uses for walnuts have been in sweet dishes and in cakes and biscuits but they are also very successful if used in bread, sauces, and in salads – Waldorf Salad, for example. Ground nuts add interest to nut roasts, stuffings and rissoles.

Seeds

There are a variety of seeds on sale, particularly in health food shops, which can add a lot of interest to vegetarian cooking. These include sesame seeds, pumpkin seeds and sunflower seeds. They are usually sold hulled and ready to use, though some pumpkin seeds may need the husks removing. Sesame seeds can be bought already ground into a paste. This is known as tahini. Sunflower seeds also provide sunflower oil which is high in polyunsaturated fats.

Nutrition. All of these seeds contain high levels of both protein and fat with little or no carbohydrates. Sesame seeds are particularly rich in calcium and also offer iron, vitamin A and the B group of vitamins. Their calorie counts are as follows: sesame seeds 100 calories per 25 g/1 oz, sunflower seeds 170 calories per 25 g/1 oz, and pumpkin seeds 173 calories per 25 g/1 oz.

Preparation. These seeds are relatively small and can be used whole or ground. They can also be toasted by spreading out on the grill pan under a low heat. Turn frequently and take care not to burn them.

Uses. Seeds are extremely versatile and can be used in both sweet and savoury dishes. Try sunflower seeds or pumpkin seeds in muesli, sprinkled on salads or vegetables and in stuffings and nut mixes. Toasted sesame seeds make an excellent topping for bread and cakes and they can also be used to flavour dips and other dishes. Greek Humous, for example, uses chick peas with tahini.

Cereals

BARLEY
Though more usually nowadays fed to cattle or used in the production of malt, barley has a deliciously creamy and nutty flavour. It does not require any form of soaking and can be used in a variety of dishes. It is quite quick to cook.

Pot or Scotch barley is on sale in health food shops. This is whole barley with the outer husks removed. Pearl barley which is on sale in most supermarkets is similar but it has had more of the skin removed and is therefore more highly polished.

Flaked barley is also available from health food shops. This varies in its degree of coarseness and you may need to experiment with different brands.

Nutrition. Pot and flaked barley retain all the nutrients of the grain, but pearl barley has lost 70 percent of its vitamin B content and a good deal of its mineral content. Protein, carbohydrate and fat levels are similar to other cereals. Barley contains good levels of dietary fibre and also calcium, iron and phosphorous. The gluten content of barley protein is much lower than that of wheat, so barley flour usually needs to be mixed with wheat flour to bake satisfactory bread or cakes.

Preparation. Wash pot barley and cook in about three times its own volume of liquid. Use a heavy-based pan with a well-fitting lid. Simmer for about 50 minutes to 1 hour or until all the liquid has been absorbed and the grains are tender. Alternatively bake in a covered casserole in the oven. This may take a little longer. Flavour by cooking with any kind of lightly fried vegetables such as onions, peas, mushrooms or peppers or cook in tomato juice or coconut milk. The barley may also be fried before cooking.

Cook flaked barley in the top of a double saucepan. Allow three to four times its own volume of liquid depending on how thick a porridge you require. Alternatively bake in the oven.

To toast flaked barley, spread the flakes out on the grill pan and toast under a low grill, turning from time to time.

To make barley water scald 75 g/3 oz barley with boiling water and drain. Place in a pan and cover with 2.4 l/4 pints water. Bring to the boil and cook until the water is reduced by half. Strain and serve with lemon juice and sugar to taste.

Uses. Serve pot barley as an accompaniment to the main course of the meal or use in stuffings and soup. Flaked barley makes a good pudding in its own right. Flavour with dried or fresh fruit. Or purée the porridge and use as a base for sweet or savoury mousses, moulds and pâtés. Use plain or toasted flakes in muesli.

BUCKWHEAT (KASHA)

Buckwheat is a staple food in Russia and in the Slav countries. The grains are small and when cooked have a very distinctive flavour and a rather mushy texture. It can be bought raw or roasted. The latter is known as kasha from the cereal's Russian name. Raw buckwheat must be roasted before use. Buckwheat is not really a true cereal but because it can be ground to a meal which can be used in bread-making it is often regarded as one.

Both whole grain buckwheat and buckwheat flour can be bought in health food shops and the flour in some supermarkets. Soba or Japanese buckwheat noodles can be bought in some health food shops and in specialist Chinese and Japanese delicatessens.

Nutrition. Buckwheat is rich in protein. Buckwheat flour has a calorie count of 95 calories per 25 g/1 oz.

Preparation. Roast raw buckwheat grains by spreading in a hot frying pan, either dry in a non-stick pan or with a little oil, and stir over a medium heat until evenly browned.

To cook buckwheat place in a saucepan with two and a half times its own volume of liquid. Bring to the boil, season and cook over a very low heat for 20–30 minutes or until all the liquid has been absorbed and the buckwheat is soft and a little mushy, or bake in a moderate oven. If you prefer, the buckwheat can be cooked in a steamer. This may take a little longer but you will be able to catch it just as it changes from being too chewy and before it gets too mushy.

Uses. Serve buckwheat with vegetables or with beans. Press into rissoles with a variety of other ingredients and shallow or deep-fry. Use in stuffings and nut loaves.

Buckwheat flour can be used in batters and pancakes; in the very fine Japanese tempura-type of batter the buckwheat flour exerts a binding effect so that eggs can be dispensed with. The flour can also be used in bread, cakes and biscuits but only sparingly for it tends to impart a rather earthy flavour to the food.

BULGAR AND CRACKED WHEAT

These are preparations of wheat which are much used in Middle Eastern cookery. Cracked wheat is made by drying the wheat and cracking it. Bulgar is boiled and then dried and cracked. It comes in varying degrees of coarseness. They are quick and easy to cook and make good substitutes for rice. Bulgar can be soaked and used without cooking. They are both on sale in most health food stores.

Nutrition. The nutritional content of these products is similar to that of wheat (see page 22).

Preparation. Cook either bulgar or cracked wheat in twice their volume of liquid. Bring to the boil, cover with a lid and reduce the heat. Leave to simmer for about 15–20 minutes. Do not lift the lid or stir until the cereal is cooked, then fluff up with a fork.

Both these cereals can also be cooked in the oven or they can be steamed. Allow a little more time for each of these methods. They can also be fried with other vegetables and then cooked.

Uses. Serve as an alternative to rice or potatoes. Use instead of rice to make pilaffs and risottos. Use in stuffings and vegetable fillings. Sweet applications include bread, cakes and baked desserts.

CORN OR MAIZE

This takes in fresh, frozen and canned corn-on-the-cob or sweetcorn and coarse yellow cornmeal or polenta, as well as the very much finer maizemeal and cornflour which come from a variety of corn. They are all available, except perhaps the maizemeal, in general grocers and supermarkets. Popcorn is a form of dried corn and cornflakes are made from refined corn.

Whole maizemeal is simply ground from the whole grain and is the most nutritious. The more commonly available products are made from grain from which the oil has been extracted and some may be even further refined. Corn oil is common on most supermarket shelves. It is particularly good for deep-frying.

Nutrition. Popcorn and ground corn or maize products offer quite high levels of protein, but the protein contains no gluten which means that it is not possible to make leavened bread with corn. It does mean, however, that the cereal can be used in a gluten-free diet. Popcorn or maizemeal, of course, contain the highest fat levels. Corn is deficient in nicotinic acid, one of the B complex vitamins, and because of this in some countries it is associated with pellagra. However in those countries in which a fully balanced diet is available the deficiency is irrelevant. Yellow maize but not white contains vitamin A.

Fresh sweetcorn offers plenty of dietary fibre and some vitamin C but, of course, has a much lower protein and fat content offering mainly carbohydrates.

Calorie counts for 25 g/1 oz are as follows: fresh sweetcorn 35 calories, frozen sweetcorn 28 calories, canned sweetcorn 22 calories, popcorn 95 calories, maizemeal 90 calories, cornmeal 90 calories, cornflour 90 calories and cornflakes 90 calories.

Preparation. Fresh sweetcorn cooks very quickly and if it is overcooked it will go tough. Place whole cobs or kernels in plenty of water and cook for about 8–10 minutes. Serve with butter and herbs. Or wrap in foil or leave in its husk and bake in the oven or on the barbecue. These methods will take a little longer.

Popcorn is dropped into a saucepan with a little hot oil on the bottom, covered tightly and shaken over the heat. The corn will begin to pop when it gets hot. Serve with butter or honey or tamari for flavouring.

To make cornmeal porridge or polenta, allow about 3–4 times the volume of water to cornmeal. Bring the water to the boil and pour in the cornmeal in a thin but steady stream, whisking well with a fork to prevent any lumps forming. If possible use a non-stick pan. Continue cooking and stirring until the mixture thickens. Leave to cook over a low heat for 15–20 minutes, stirring occasionally.

Uses. Cornflour and maizemeal may be used as thickening agents in sauces, soups, soufflés, mousses and moulds or they may be used with other kinds of flour to make a variety of breads, cakes and biscuits. They tend to make very short shortbread and light crumbly pastry.

Cornmeal makes excellent puddings and porridges. In Italy it is used to make polenta which can be served on its own or be mixed with spinach, cheese, tomatoes, or other flavourings. A similar dish is made in Africa and in the Caribbean and here it may be flavoured with okra, peanuts or chilli peppers.

Fresh sweetcorn can be eaten on its own either on or off the cob or used in any kind of fresh vegetable dish. It also goes well in soups, stews, risottos and pilaffs.

COUSCOUS

This is an Arab dish usually made from the inner layers of the wheat grain. However, whole wheat couscous can be bought from some health food stores. It looks a little like bulgar.

Nutrition. Whole grain couscous should have about the same food value as whole wheat itself.

Preparation. The best method is to steam couscous in a special steamer. However, it can also be cooked on the top of the stove. Start by lightly roasting the couscous in a dry pan, stirring continuously. Pour on sufficient boiling water to cover the top of the couscous by about 5 mm–1 cm/¼–½ in. Season and bring to the boil. Either simmer very gently over an extremely low heat or turn off the heat altogether and leave the couscous to swell up and cook in its own heat. This will take about 20 minutes. The finished dish should be light, dry and fluffy.

Uses. Serve in place of rice or potatoes. Mix with other vegetables and flavourings such as ginger, spring onions or garlic for a change.

MILLET
Millet is eaten extensively in Africa and in the East but is far less well known in Europe. Whole millet is available at health food stores, as is flaked millet.

Nutrition. Millet offers a similar protein, fat and carbohydrate profile to other cereals. Like corn its protein make-up lacks gluten which means that it can be used in a gluten-free diet.

Preparation. Whole millet may be cooked as it is or it may be roasted first. To do this fry in a very little oil until lightly browned and giving off a delicious nutty smell. Add two to two and a half times its volume of liquid and bring to the boil. Simmer very gently for about 30 minutes or until all the liquid has been absorbed and the millet is light and fluffy. Millet can also be baked in a moderate oven but this will take a little longer. Add chopped and sautéed vegetables as desired.

Flaked millet should be cooked in about three to four times its volume of liquid depending on how thick you want the resulting porridge. Cook in the top of a double saucepan for about 30–40 minutes, stirring from time to time.

Uses. Serve millet in place of rice or potatoes or use to make stuffings, salads and vegetarian baked loaves or rissoles. Use flaked millet to coat loaves and rissoles or use to make milk puddings and moulds.

OATS

This traditional northern food is available in a variety of forms on the supermarket shelves. Porridge oats are probably the most popular. These are flaked or rolled oats. Some of the brands are known as quick porridge oats, others as pinhead (small) or jumbo (large) flakes. Flaked oats are made from whole grain oats or groats which have been lightly steamed and roasted to stabilise them.

Oats also come as oatmeal and this is ground fine, medium or coarse from the whole grain. Because it has not been stabilised it may grow bitter with age. Whole grain oats or groats may also be bought at the health food shop.

Nutrition. Oats contain more fat than some of the other cereals but they are equally rich in protein. Only the husk is removed in milling and oatmeal retains most of its fibre and all the nutrients of the germ. Oats contain iron but to get the most benefit from this the oats should be eaten with a food which is rich in Vitamin C such as oranges or grapefruit. They also contain potassium, calcium, phosphorous and the B group of vitamins.

Preparation. In Scotland porridge is traditionally made with oatmeal. Slowly add one part of medium oatmeal to four and a half parts of very hot salty water, stirring with the straight end of a wooden spoon. Bring to the boil, stirring all the time, and simmer for 30 minutes. Flakes will cook rather faster than this. Toast the oatmeal and flakes for a change in flavour. Porridge can also be made in the top of a double saucepan.

Whole oats or groats should be soaked in twice their own volume of liquid and cooked in the same way as whole barley or soaked whole wheat grains. Flavour with herbs, spices and vegetables such as onion, ginger or garlic.

Uses. In addition to porridge, oats can be used to thicken all kinds of stews and sauces. They form an important part of a muesli base and can also be used in crumble toppings, coatings for fried and baked foods and in stuffings.

Both oatmeal and oat flakes can be used to flavour bread, cakes, biscuits and pastry. Flapjack is traditionally made with rolled oats.

Whole grain oats can be served in place of rice or potatoes. They can be mixed with other whole grains or with bulgar or millet to give a variation in texture and flavour.

RICE

This is one of the staple cereals of the world and there are numerous books devoted to it. Because of this it has not been widely used in this book. However, whole brown rice could be used in any of the recipes for whole grain oats, barley or wheat; flaked rice can be used in all of the recipes for flaked millet and barley and most of the recipes for rolled or flaked oats; ground rice can be used for any recipe using coarse ground cornmeal or polenta and rice flour for all recipes using maizemeal.

RYE

Whole rye is difficult to find. However, it can be used in much the same way as whole wheat and it also needs to be soaked before use. Rye flour is available from some supermarkets and most health food stores. The flour is used mainly in bread and biscuits. Rye flakes can also be bought in health food stores.

WHEAT

Wheat is, of course, the staple cereal of the West and whole-wheat flour is available in every supermarket. Whole grain wheat is only on sale in health food shops as is flaked wheat.

Wholewheat is also used to make cracked wheat and bulgar and some couscous and semolina.

Nutrition. In the average British diet wheat supplies a quarter of the total protein. It also offers dietary fibre, vitamins of the B group, vitamin E and a variety of minerals.

Preparation. Whole grain wheat must be soaked in cold water overnight before use. Otherwise it will be almost impossible to chew – even after extensive cooking. This process can be speeded up a little by pouring on hot water and leaving to stand for two hours before use but the cooked wheat will still be chewier than if it had been soaked overnight.

Drain the wheat after soaking and then cook in two to three times its own volume of liquid. Bring to the boil, cover and simmer for about 45 minutes to 1 hour. Cook with different flavourings such as tomato juice, herbs or spices and add vegetables to taste.

Wheat flakes may be cooked in the top of a double pan in just the same way as barley or oatflakes. Allow about 45 minutes cooking time and add three to four times the volume of milk or other liquid depending on how thick you require the resultant mixture to be.

Uses. The main use of wholewheat flour is in bread, cake, biscuits and pastry making and in thickening soups, sauces and stews. It is also used to make wholewheat pasta.

Wholegrain wheat may be served in place of potatoes or rice. It can also be used in salads and stuffings. Wheat flakes are used in muesli and to make porridge and milk puddings.

Other Ingredients Used

GELOZONE
This is a vegetable setting agent and is available from health food shops.

QUARK
This is a low-fat soft cheese available in most supermarkets.

TOFU
This is a bean curd made from soya milk. It is available in a fresh form and as silken tofu, which is softer and is packaged in long-life cartons. They are both available from health food shops.

CHAPTER TWO

Starters

Buckwheat Blintzes

Pastry
175 g/6 oz wholemeal flour,
  sifted
50 g/2 oz buckwheat
1 teaspoon salt

1 tablespoon cooking oil
2 eggs, beaten
4 tablespoons water

Filling
1 large onion, finely chopped
1 tablespoon cooking oil
25 g/1 oz toasted buckwheat
75–100 ml/3–4 fl oz water,
  mixed with ½ teaspoon yeast
  extract

50 g/2 oz frozen peas, thawed
2 hard-boiled eggs, chopped
¼ teaspoon mixed dried herbs
salt and pepper

Mix the flour, buckwheat and salt in a bowl. Add the cooking oil, beaten eggs and sufficient water to make a stiff paste. Roll out as thinly as possible between sheets of greaseproof paper or baking parchment. Set aside.

To make the filling, fry the onion in the cooking oil until lightly browned. Add the toasted buckwheat and stir well together. Transfer to a double saucepan, pour on the water and yeast mixture and bring to the boil. Reduce the heat and simmer for 30–40 minutes until the buckwheat is soft.

Stir in all the remaining filling ingredients, with seasoning to taste.

Cut the pastry into eight squares and dampen the edges with water. Place spoonfuls of the filling in the centre of each square and fold the pastry over to form triangular shapes. Pinch the pastry well together to seal. Bake on a greased tray at 180°C/350°F/Gas 4 for 15–20 minutes.

Rye Blinis with Curried Soured Cream

Buckwheat can be used in place of rye.

1 teaspoon dried yeast
300 ml/½ pt pint warm milk
50 g/2 oz wholemeal flour, sifted
50 g/2 oz rye flour
pinch salt

1 egg, separated
1 tablespoon single cream
½ teaspoon mild curry powder
150 ml/¼ pint soured cream

Mix the yeast with half the milk and leave in a warm place for 20 minutes. Gradually add enough of the wholemeal and rye flours to the yeast mixture to make a stiffish dough. Cover with a cloth and leave to rise in a warm place for 2 hours.

Mix the remaining flour into the risen dough with the salt, egg yolk, remaining milk and single cream. Beat the egg white stiffly and fold into the batter. Leave to rise again for 30 minutes.

Meanwhile, mix the curry powder with the soured cream and leave to stand.

To cook the blinis, grease a small pancake or crêpe pan with a very little fat and heat the pan. Pour in sufficient batter just to cover the bottom of the pan. Cook until the underside of the blini is brown. Turn it over and cook the second side. Tip the blini out of the pan, and keep hot while you continue making more blinis in the same way. Serve hot with the curried soured cream.

Onions Stuffed with Pistachios

Serve with tomato sauce (see page 28).

4 large onions, peeled and left whole
75 g/3 oz fresh wholemeal breadcrumbs
75 g/3 oz pistachio nuts, roasted, shelled and chopped
salt and pepper

Steam the onions in a steamer or in a very little boiling water until they are soft enough to push out the centres. Chop the centres very finely and mix with the breadcrumbs, nuts and seasoning to taste. Press the filling mixture into the onions, piling it up on the top.

Place the onions in a casserole dish. Cover and bake at 200°C/400°F/Gas 6 for 30 minutes. Remove the lid and bake for a further 15 minutes to allow the tops to brown. Serve with a little tomato sauce or spiced yogurt.

Spiced Millet with Peanut Sauce

This dish makes an unusual starter but it can also be served as part of the main course.

1 onion, very finely chopped
1 clove garlic, crushed
1 cm/½ in piece fresh root
  ginger, grated
½ green pepper, seeded and
  chopped
1 tablespoon cooking oil

225 g/8 oz whole millet
2 teaspoons miso, mixed with
  600 ml/1 pint water or
  vegetable stock
salt and pepper

Sauce
300 ml/½ pint milk
4 tablespoons peanut butter

1 tablespoon soy sauce
1 teaspoon lemon juice

Fry the onion, garlic, ginger and green pepper in the cooking oil for 2–3 minutes until the onion turns transparent. Stir in the millet, then add the miso and water or vegetable stock and seasoning to taste. Bring the mixture to the boil. Reduce the heat as low as possible, cover and cook very gently for 30 minutes or until all the liquid has been absorbed and the millet is soft and fluffy.

Meanwhile, to make the peanut sauce, carefully stir the milk into the peanut butter in a saucepan over a low heat. Stir in the soy sauce and lemon juice. Heat through but do not allow to boil. Serve the millet with the peanut sauce.

Spinach Gnocchi with Tomato Sauce

225 g/8 oz frozen chopped
   spinach
350 ml/12 fl oz milk
25 g/1 oz butter or margarine
40 g/1½ oz yellow cornmeal or
   polenta

pinch grated nutmeg
salt
50 g/2 oz Parmesan cheese,
   grated (optional)

Sauce
1 × 400 g/14 oz can tomatoes
2 tablespoons tomato purée
1 small onion, grated

½ teaspoon sugar
pinch salt

Thaw the spinach in a non-stick pan and cook for a few minutes to evaporate all the liquid. Add the milk, butter or margarine and cornmeal or polenta and bring to the boil, stirring all the time. When the mixture thickens, reduce the heat. Stir in the nutmeg and salt to taste and cook gently for 10–15 minutes, stirring from time to time. Leave to cool.

Meanwhile, place all the sauce ingredients in another saucepan and bring to the boil. Simmer for about 10 minutes to thicken a little. Purée or rub through a sieve.

When the spinach mixture is cool, shape it with a spoon into 8 cakes and place on 4 ovenproof dishes. Spoon the tomato sauce over the top and sprinkle with the Parmesan cheese, if using. Bake at 200°C/400°F/Gas 6 for 15–20 minutes.

Tomatoes Stuffed with Herb Millet

This dish makes a good starter or it can be served as an accompaniment to steaks and grills instead of potatoes or rice.

75 g/3 oz whole millet	25 g/1 oz pine nuts, chopped
6 spring onions, finely chopped	2 tablespoons freshly chopped
¼ teaspoon mixed dried herbs	parsley
1 vegetable stock cube	salt and pepper
200 ml/8 fl oz boiling water	4 large continental tomatoes

Place the millet, spring onions and herbs in a small saucepan. Dissolve the stock cube in the boiling water and pour over the millet. Bring to the boil, then reduce the heat as low as it will go. Cover the pan and cook very gently for 30 minutes or until all the liquid has been absorbed and the millet is soft and fluffy. Leave to cool.

Meanwhile, place the pine nuts in a dry frying pan over a good heat and toast until they are lightly browned. Mix the pine nuts into the cool millet with the parsley and seasoning to taste.

Cut the tops off the tomatoes. Scoop out the centres and the seeds with a teaspoon and discard. Fill the tomatoes with the millet mixture and place in an ovenproof dish. Bake at 180°C/ 350°F/Gas 4 for 10–15 minutes.

Nut Butter

Nut butters are very easily made in the food processor. Once made they can be thinned with a little oil and flavoured with herbs, spices and vegetables for savoury applications or they can be mixed with fruit purées, chopped dates or bananas to make cake fillings, sweet spreads or fruit stuffings.

Suitable nuts are hazelnuts, walnuts and peanuts. Cashew nuts can also be used but they tend to remain much dryer without the addition of extra oil.

225 g/8 oz nuts
a little cooking or nut oil

Remove the skins from the nuts if necessary and blend in a food processor for a few minutes until the ground nuts start to exude their oils and stick together. Add a little more oil at this stage if necessary.

Hazelnut Dip with Crudités

225 g/8 oz hazelnut butter (see pages 29–30)
3 tablespoons silken tofu or quark
2–3 teaspoons lemon juice
salt and pepper

Crudités
2 carrots, cut into sticks
2 bunches spring onions, trimmed
7.5 cm/3 in piece cucumber, cut into sticks
1 small head cauliflower, broken into florets

Place the hazelnut butter, tofu or quark, lemon juice and seasoning to taste in a blender or food processor and blend to a smooth creamy texture. Transfer to a bowl and surround with the prepared crudités.

Stuffed Mushrooms

50 g/2 oz dates, stoned
100 g/4 oz cashew nut butter
  made without oil (see pages
  29–30)
1½ tablespoons silken tofu or
  quark

salt and pepper
175 g/6 oz small button
  mushrooms
16–20 raisins
parsley sprigs

Add the dates to the nut butter in the food processor and continue processing until well mixed. Add the tofu or quark and seasoning to taste.

Cut the stalks out of the mushrooms. Spoon a little of the cashew nut mixture inside the buttons. Decorate each one with a raisin and a small sprig of parsley.

Celery Stuffed with Avocado Nut Dip

If you are in a hurry the avocado nut dip can be served surrounded with the celery sticks to use as dippers.

1 ripe avocado, peeled and stoned
juice of ½ lemon
100 g/4 oz hazelnut butter (see pages 29–30)
50 g/2 oz cream cheese
6–8 sticks celery, cut into lengths
1 teaspoon chopped dry-roasted sunflower seeds

Purée the avocado and lemon juice in a blender or food processor or rub through a sieve. Mix with the hazelnut butter and the cream cheese until a smooth creamy paste is formed. Spoon into celery lengths and top with the sunflower seeds.

Spiced Walnut Canapés

100 g/4 oz walnut butter (see pages 29–30)
1½ tablespoons silken tofu or quark
2 teaspoons grated fresh root ginger
salt and pepper
6 slices wholemeal bread, fried in cooking oil
6 whole walnuts, shelled and chopped

Place the nut butter, tofu or quark, ginger, and salt and pepper to taste in a blender or food processor and blend well together. Spread over the cold fried bread and cut into small squares. Decorate each square with a small piece of chopped walnut.

Shropka with Nuts

Use dry-roasted cashew nuts or pine nuts if you do not want to use salted peanuts. Vegans omit the cheese.

4 tomatoes, coarsely chopped
10 cm/4 in piece cucumber, diced
3 sticks celery, sliced
½ green pepper, seeded and chopped
1 small onion, chopped

50 g/2 oz dry-roasted salted peanuts
juice of 1 lemon
75 g/3 oz Gouda cheese, grated
freshly ground black pepper

Mix all the vegetables with the nuts and toss with lemon juice. Spoon into four individual bowls and sprinkle with the cheese and pepper to taste. Chill for 30 minutes before serving.

Avocado Salad with Toasted Peanuts

2 large ripe avocados, peeled and
  stoned
freshly ground black pepper
lime juice
4 tomatoes, peeled and chopped
1 onion, finely chopped
2 green peppers, seeded and
  sliced

75 g/3 oz unsalted peanuts,
  toasted under the grill
2 tablespoons mayonnaise
1 tablespoon chutney
shredded lettuce
sliced cucumber

Chop the avocado and sprinkle with black pepper and lime juice to taste. Add the tomatoes, onion, green peppers and peanuts. Stir in the mayonnaise and chutney. Serve on a bed of shredded lettuce, garnished with cucumber slices.

Tabouli

This deliciously refreshing salad can be eaten on lettuce leaves or with pitta bread. It is served throughout the Middle East as part of the *mezze* or selection of starter dishes.

75 g/3 oz bulgar
10 cm/4 in piece cucumber, very
  finely chopped
3 tomatoes, peeled and very
  finely chopped
1 small green pepper, seeded and
  finely chopped
1 small onion or bunch spring
  onions, very finely chopped

3 tablespoons freshly chopped
  parsley
1 tablespoon freshly chopped
  mint
juice of 2 lemons
2 tablespoons olive oil
salt and pepper

Wash the bulgar and leave to soak in 175 ml/6 fl oz water for 1 hour. Drain and squeeze out all the water from the bulgar. Leave to stand for about 10 minutes, then squeeze again. Mix with all the remaining ingredients. Chill for 30 minutes. Before serving, pour off any more liquid which might have collected.

Mushroom and Barley Pâté

2 onions, finely chopped
450 g/1 lb mushrooms, very
  finely chopped
3 tablespoons vegetable cooking
  oil
25 g/1 oz flaked barley, ground
150 ml/¼ pint milk
50 g/2 oz ground almonds

50 g/2 oz fresh wholemeal
  breadcrumbs
2 eggs
a few drops Tabasco sauce
2 teaspoons dried oregano
salt and pepper

Fry the onions and mushrooms in the cooking oil until soft. Set aside. Place the barley in a double saucepan with the milk and cook for 40 minutes or until most of the liquid has been absorbed and the barley is cooked. Drain off any excess liquid. Stir in the fried vegetables and all the remaining ingredients.

Spoon into a 450 g/1 lb loaf tin and place in a baking tray filled with 2 cm/1 in hot water. Bake at 180°C/350°F/Gas 4 for 1 hour.

Mushroom and Brazil Nut Cheese

1 small onion, finely chopped
25 g/1 oz butter or firm
  margarine
225 g/8 oz button mushrooms,
  finely chopped
125 g/5 oz plain yogurt
100 g/4 oz curd cheese
3 tablespoons freshly chopped
  parsley

75 g/3 oz Brazil nuts, finely
  chopped
salt and pepper
3 teaspoons Gelozone
1½ tablespoons sherry
2 tablespoons lemon juice
sliced button mushrooms to
  garnish
parsley sprigs

Gently fry the onion in the butter or margarine until softened, then add the mushrooms. Fry gently until the mushrooms soften. Stir in the yogurt, cheese, parsley and nuts and season to taste with salt and pepper. Remove from the heat.

Mix the Gelozone with the sherry and lemon juice in a small saucepan and bring to the boil. Simmer gently for 1 minute, then add to the mushroom and cheese mixture. Mix well together. Spoon into individual ramekin dishes or into one larger mould and leave to cool. Chill for 2 hours or until set. Serve turned out, garnished with sliced mushrooms and parsley.

Chestnut Party Dip

To vary the flavour of this unusual dip use curry powder in place of the spices specified.

1 × 439 g/1 lb can whole *pinch mixed spices*
 unsweetened chestnuts *salt and pepper*
450 g/1 lb quark *celery and carrot sticks to serve*
1 teaspoon ground cumin
1 teaspoon ground coriander

Drain the chestnuts, reserving 4 tablespoons of the liquid from the can. Purée the chestnuts in a blender or food processor or rub through a sieve. Mix in the quark a little at a time, then add the reserved juice from the can of chestnuts. Mix to a smooth cream. Stir in the spices and salt and pepper to taste and mix well together. Turn into a bowl and surround with the raw vegetable dippers.

Savoury Nut and Cheese Fingers

Serve this delicious cocktail snack on its own or with cheese or avocado dips.

100 g/4 oz wholemeal flour
50 g/2 oz hazelnuts, very finely chopped
25 g/1 oz cheese, grated
75 g/3 oz butter, cut into small pieces

Sift the flour into a bowl to remove some of the bran. Stir in the
nuts and cheese. Rub in the butter and press the mixture
together to make a stiff but sticky dough. Roll out on a
well-floured board and cut into 20–30 sticks or fingers. Place on
a baking tray and bake at 180°C/350°F/Gas 4 for about 25
minutes or until lightly browned.

Corn and Egg Tartlets

Pastry

75 g/3 oz wholemeal flour, sifted   pinch salt
50 g/2 oz fine maizemeal   100 g/4 oz firm margarine, cut
25 g/1 oz medium cornmeal or   into small pieces
   polenta   1 egg yolk

Filling

6 tablespoons milk   freshly ground black pepper
large knob of butter   225 g/8 oz sweetcorn kernels,
6 eggs, beaten   frozen or canned
1 teaspoon dried tarragon,
   crushed

Place all the dry ingredients for the pastry in a bowl. Add the
margarine and rub into the dry ingredients until the mixture
resembles fine breadcrumbs. Bind with the egg yolk. Roll out
the dough and use to line 16 tart or bun tins. Prick all over with
a fork and bake blind at 200°C/400°F/Gas 6 for 15 minutes or
until crisp. Leave to cool a little, then transfer to a wire rack to
cool.

To make the filling, heat the milk and butter in a saucepan
and add the eggs. Stir until the eggs are lightly scrambled. Stir
in the tarragon and pepper to taste and leave to cool. Cook
frozen corn as directed on the packet and leave to cool, or drain
canned corn. Mix into the eggs and use to fill the cold tartlet
cases.

Nut and Sesame Savouries

Serve as pre-dinner appetisers or as part of a cocktail buffet.

75 g/3 oz Cheddar cheese, grated
25 g/1 oz roasted nuts (cashews
* and peanuts), chopped*
2 tablespoons raisins, chopped
2 tablespoons mayonnaise

1 teaspoon lemon juice
salt and pepper
4 slices wholemeal bread
1 tablespoon sesame seeds

Mix the cheese, nuts, raisins, mayonnaise and lemon juice in a bowl and season to taste with salt and pepper. Chill for 1 hour.

Toast the bread lightly on both sides. Spread with the nut and cheese mixture, sprinkle with sesame seeds and place under a hot grill to brown. Cut each slice into 6 squares and serve at once.

CHAPTER THREE

Soups

Carrot and Oatmeal Soup with Orange

1 onion, sliced
1 tablespoon cooking oil
2 tablespoons oatmeal
3 tablespoons sherry (optional)

900 ml/1½ pints vegetable stock
made with 2 vegetable stock
cubes
450 g/1 lb carrots, sliced
1 large orange

Gently fry the onion in the cooking oil for 2–3 minutes or until the onion turns translucent. Stir in the oatmeal and then the sherry if used. Next stir in a little of the vegetable stock and bring to the boil. Gradually add the rest of the stock and return to the boil. Add the carrots and simmer for 30 minutes.

Purée in a blender or food processor with the chopped rind and flesh of the orange, or sieve with the orange flesh and stir in the grated rind. Reheat and serve.

Sprout and Chestnut Soup

If using canned chestnuts check to see that they are un-sweetened!

1 onion, chopped
1 tablespoon cooking oil
450 g/1 lb Brussels sprouts, sliced
100 g/4 oz chestnuts, shelled and sliced, or 75 g/3 oz canned chestnuts, drained and sliced

300 ml/½ pint milk or soya milk
600 ml/1 pint vegetable stock
pinch mixed dried herbs
salt and pepper

Fry the onion in the cooking oil until well browned. Add all the remaining ingredients and bring to the boil. Reduce the heat, cover and simmer for 30 minutes. Purée in a blender or food processor, or rub through a sieve. Reheat and serve.

Peanut Soup

The use of milk in this recipe gives a smoother, creamier soup but vegans may wish to omit it.

1 onion, very finely chopped
3 sticks celery, chopped
1 tablespoon cooking oil
25 g/1 oz ground unsalted raw peanuts
1 tablespoon wholemeal flour

750 ml/1¼ pints vegetable stock or half vegetable stock and half milk
3 tablespoons peanut butter
salt and pepper
chopped peanuts to garnish

Gently fry the onion and celery in the cooking oil for 2–3 minutes or until they begin to soften. Stir in the ground nuts and flour and then the stock or stock and milk. Bring to the boil and simmer for 30 minutes.

Stir in the peanut butter and salt and pepper to taste and reheat. Do not allow the mixture to boil. Serve with a few chopped peanuts sprinkled over the top.

Swiss Barley Soup

I first tried this soup at the Swiss Centre in London and was so keen on it I worked out the ingredients for myself. Serve with thinly sliced cheese and wholemeal bread.

40 g/1½ oz whole grain or pot barley, washed and drained
1 onion, finely chopped
600 ml/1 pint vegetable stock, made with 1 vegetable stock cube
450 ml/¾ pint milk
salt and pepper

Place all the ingredients in a saucepan and bring to the boil. Reduce the heat and simmer, covered, for 1 hour.

Borsch with Buchwheat Kasha

3 uncooked beetroot, grated
1 × 400 g/14 oz can tomatoes
1 stick celery, finely chopped
1 onion, finely chopped
1 bay leaf
175 g/6 oz green cabbage,
  shredded

2 medium-sized potatoes, diced
900 ml/1½ pints water
salt and pepper
baked kasha (see page 71)
soured cream

Place the beetroot in a saucepan with the tomatoes. Add the celery, onion and bay leaf and simmer for 10 minutes. Add the cabbage, potatoes and water. Season to taste with salt and pepper. Simmer for 1 hour or until the vegetables are tender. Serve with a tablespoon of baked kasha in each plate and a swirl of soured cream.

Corn Chowder

Either soya milk or dairy milk may be used in this recipe, but the former gives a fuller, 'creamier' effect.

1 onion, finely chopped	100 g/4 oz frozen peas
2 medium-sized potatoes, diced	450 ml/¾ pint vegetable stock
kernels from 2 corn on the cob, or about 100 g/4 oz frozen or canned sweetcorn kernels	450 ml/¾ pint soya or dairy milk
	salt and pepper

Place all the ingredients in a saucepan and bring to the boil. Cover and simmer very gently for 20–30 minutes or until all the vegetables are tender.

Thick Cereal and Split Pea Soup

This is very much a meal in itself!

1 large onion, chopped	175 g/6 oz whole grain wheat, soaked for 2 hours and drained, or pot barley
1 tablespoon cooking oil	
1 large carrot, chopped	
3 sticks celery, chopped	75 g/3 oz flaked barley
1 tablespoon yeast extract	1 bay leaf
1.2 litres/2 pints water	1 teaspoon dried marjoram
100 g/4 oz dried split peas, soaked for 2 hours in cold water and drained	½ teaspoon dried savory
	pepper

Fry the onion in the cooking oil until it turns translucent. Add the carrot and celery and continue frying for a further 2–3 minutes. Add all the remaining ingredients and bring to the boil. Cover and simmer for about 1½ hours, stirring from time to time. If the mixture gets too thick or starts to stick to the bottom of the pan, add a little more water.

CHAPTER FOUR

Main Course Dishes

Cashew Nut Pastry Flan with Beans and Tomatoes

Toast the ground nuts in a dry non-stick frying pan until well browned. This is also very good made with peanuts.

Pastry

50 g/2 oz butter or firm margarine
100 g/4 oz wholemeal flour
salt

50 g/2 oz ground cashew nuts, toasted
1 tablespoon water

Filling

1 large onion, chopped
1 tablespoon cooking oil
450 g/1 lb tomatoes, peeled and chopped
1 teaspoon sugar

1 × 213g/7 oz can butter beans, drained
100 g/4 oz hard cheese, grated
salt and pepper

Place the flour and salt in a bowl and rub in the fat until the mixture resembles fine breadcrumbs. Stir in the toasted cashew nuts and bind with the water. Press the pastry into a 20 cm/8 in loose-bottomed flan tin.

Fry the onion in the cooking oil until soft. Stir in the tomatoes and continue cooking for 5 minutes. Add the sugar. Remove from the heat and stir in the butter beans, half the cheese and salt and pepper to taste. Spoon into the flan case. Sprinkle the remaining cheese over the top.

Bake at 190°C/375°F/Gas 5 for 20 minutes or until the pastry is cooked and the cheese on top is well browned.

Nut and Vegetable Party Flan

Toast the pine nuts under the grill before chopping. For a shorter pastry substitute 25 g/1 oz fine oatmeal or maizemeal for the same quantity of flour.

Pastry

150 g/5 oz wholemeal flour, sifted	65 g/2½ oz butter or firm margarine
salt	1 egg, beaten

Filling

4 sticks celery, sliced	150 ml/¼ pint single cream
1 onion, sliced	2 eggs
1 tablespoon cooking oil	75 ml/3 fl oz milk
50 g/2 oz toasted pine nuts or pistachio nuts, coarsely chopped	salt and pepper
	2 tomatoes, peeled and sliced
50 g/2 oz Cheddar cheese, grated	

Place the flour and salt in a bowl and rub in the fat until the mixture resembles fine breadcrumbs. Use sufficient beaten egg to bind to a firm dough. Roll or press out to line a 20 cm/8 in loose-bottomed flan tin.

Gently fry the celery and onion in the cooking oil to soften them. Brush the bottom of the pastry case with any remaining egg, then spread the celery and onion mixture over the bottom. Sprinkle with the toasted nuts and grated cheese. Mix together the cream, eggs, milk and salt and pepper to taste and pour into the pastry case. Arrange the tomato slices over the top.

Bake at 190°C/375°F/Gas 5 for 50–60 minutes or until set in the centre and lightly browned on top. Serve hot or cold.

Whole Wheat Berry Chowder with Peppers

1 onion, chopped
1 tablespoon cooking oil
1 carrot, diced
½ green pepper, seeded and diced
½ red pepper, seeded and diced
1 potato, diced
75 g/3 oz whole wheat berries, soaked overnight in cold water and drained

450 ml/¾ pint milk or soya milk
450 ml/¾ pint water
a few drops Tabasco sauce
pinch dried oregano
salt and pepper

Gently fry the onion in the cooking oil until translucent. Add the remaining vegetables and continue frying gently for 3–4 minutes. Add all the remaining ingredients and bring to the boil. Reduce the heat, cover and simmer for about 1 hour or until the wheat is tender. Add a little more milk and heat through before serving.

Ratatouille and Cornmeal Pie

1 large onion, chopped
2 tablespoons cooking oil
1 small aubergine, chopped
225 g/8 oz courgettes, diced
½ green pepper, seeded and sliced
½ red pepper, seeded and sliced
4 tomatoes, chopped

2 tablespoons tomato purée
salt and pepper
100 g/4 oz yellow cornmeal or polenta
750 ml/1¼ pints water
25 g/1 oz butter
75 g/3 oz cheese, grated (optional)

Fry the onion in the cooking oil until it turns translucent. Add all the remaining vegetables and fry gently for 5 minutes. Stir in the tomato purée and salt and pepper to taste. Continue cooking for about 40 minutes or until the ratatouille is thick and the vegetables are completely cooked through. Leave to cool a little.

Mix the cornmeal or polenta with half the water. Boil the remaining water in a pan and pour in the cornmeal and water mixture, stirring or whisking all the time. Add the butter and plenty of salt and continue stirring until the mixture thickens. Leave to simmer over a low heat for 15 minutes, stirring from time to time.

Spoon half the cornmeal mixture into a deep pie dish. Cover with the ratatouille and top this with the remaining cornmeal, adding a layer of cheese in the middle and another on top, if using cheese. Leave to stand for 15 minutes before baking at 200°C/400°F/Gas 6 for 30 minutes.

Cornmeal Flan with Cardamom Eggs

Pastry

175 g/6 oz wholemeal flour	100 g/4 oz butter or firm
50 g/2 oz yellow cornmeal or	margarine
polenta	1 egg yolk, beaten
pinch salt	a little water to bind

Filling

1 onion, finely chopped	4 hard-boiled eggs, chopped
1 tablespoon cooking oil	1 tablespoon mayonnaise
2 cardamom pods	salt and pepper
100 g/4 oz Cheddar cheese,	
grated	

Place the flour, cornmeal or polenta and salt in a bowl. Cut the fat into small pieces and rub into the dry ingredients until the mixture resembles fine breadcrumbs. Bind with the beaten egg yolk and a little water. Roll out just over half the pastry and use to line a 20 cm/8 in loose-bottomed flan tin.

Fry the onion in the cooking oil for about 5 minutes or until soft. Remove the seeds from the cardamom pods and crush. Add to the onions and mix in all the other ingredients. Use to fill the flan case.

Roll out the remaining pastry to make a lid. Cover the pie with this and stick the edges together with a little water. Prick the top all over with a fork and bake at 200°C/400°F/Gas 6 for 45 minutes to 1 hour.

Oatmeal Pepper Pie

Pastry
50 g/2 oz oatmeal
75 g/3 oz wholemeal flour
salt

50 g/2 oz firm margarine or
  butter
a little water

Filling
1 large onion, sliced
1 tablespoon cooking oil
1 large red pepper, seeded and
  sliced
4 tomatoes, peeled and chopped

1 tablespoon tomato purée
1 tablespoon oatmeal
salt and pepper
100 g/4 oz Cheddar cheese,
  grated (optional)

Mix the oatmeal, flour and salt in a bowl. Cut the fat into small pieces and rub into the dry ingredients. Bind the mixture with a little water. Roll out the pastry and use to line a 20 cm/8 in flan tin. Prick all over with a fork and bake blind at 200°C/400°F/Gas 6 for 20 minutes. Remove beans and bake for a further 10 minutes.

Meanwhile, fry the onion in the cooking oil until it turns translucent. Add the red pepper, and continue cooking for 5 minutes. Add the tomatoes, tomato purée, oatmeal, and salt and pepper to taste and cook over a low heat for 10 minutes. Use this mixture to fill the cooked pastry case.

If using cheese, sprinkle over the top and cook for 4–5 minutes under the grill to melt it.

Nutty Mushroom and Stilton Pie   Serves 6

Vegans can quite simply leave out the cheese in this delicious
and unusual recipe.

Filling
1 tablespoon cooking oil
3 sticks celery, chopped
1 bunch spring onions, chopped
250 g/9 oz open mushrooms,
    thickly sliced

3 tablespoons flour
300 ml/½ pint water
50 g/2 oz hazelnuts, chopped
salt and pepper
75 g/3 oz Stilton cheese, grated

Pastry
225 g/8 oz wholemeal flour
pinch salt
125 g/4 oz firm margarine

5 tablespoons cold water
beaten egg or milk to glaze

Heat the oil and lightly fry the celery and spring onions for
about 3 minutes. Add the mushrooms and cook for 5 minutes.
Stir in the flour and cook for 1 minute. Remove from the heat
and gradually stir in the water. Return to the heat and bring to
the boil, stirring. Add the hazelnuts and salt and pepper to
taste. Leave to cool.

To make the pastry, place the flour and salt in a bowl. Rub in
the margarine until the mixture resembles breadcrumbs, then
stir in enough water to form a not too stiff dough. Roll out just
over half the pastry and use to line a 20 cm/8 in loose-bottomed
flan tin. Moisten the pastry edges with water.

Turn the cold mushroom mixture into the flan case and
sprinkle the cheese over the top. Roll out the remaining pastry
to a large round for the lid. Cover the pie with this. Brush with
egg or milk, then bake at 200°C/400°F/Gas 6 for 50–60 minutes
or until lightly browned.

Baked Cabbage Cake

*225 g/8 oz cabbage or spring
    greens, with large leaves*
5 eggs, beaten
3 tablespoons milk
salt and pepper

25 g/1 oz butter
1 large onion, finely chopped
1 tablespoon cooking oil
100 g/4 oz bulgar or millet
250 ml/8 fl oz vegetable stock

Remove any damaged outer leaves from the cabbage and blanch all the remaining leaves in boiling water for 3 minutes. Drain and plunge into cold water. Use the large leaves to line a well-greased 600 ml/1 pint round casserole dish, allowing some of the leaves to hang over the edge. Reserve two or three large leaves for the top. Shred the remaining cabbage leaves.

Beat the eggs with the milk and salt and pepper to taste. Melt the butter in a small saucepan. Pour in the beaten eggs and stir until lightly scrambled. Remove from the heat and keep on one side.

Fry the onion in the cooking oil until translucent. Stir in the bulgar or millet and salt and pepper to taste, then pour on the stock. Bring the mixture to the boil, reduce the heat and simmer for 30 minutes or until the bulgar is fluffed up and tender.

To put the cake together spoon half the bulgar mixture into the bottom of the cabbage-lined casserole. Cover with a layer of egg and then with half the chopped cabbage. Repeat these layers again, then cover the top with the reserved large cabbage leaves and fold in the leaves which are hanging over the edge. Bake at 190°C/375°F/Gas 5 for 30 minutes. Turn out onto a heated plate to serve.

Stuffed Chinese Leaves

Almost any kind of nuts can be used in this recipe. Try almonds and pecans or pine nuts and cashews for a change of flavour.

1 head Chinese leaves
50 g/2 oz long-grain brown rice
3 tomatoes, peeled and chopped
50 g/2 oz walnuts, chopped
25 g/1 oz hazelnuts, chopped
3 tablespoons freshly chopped
  parsley

1 tablespoon freshly chopped
  chives
salt and pepper
450 ml/¾ pint vegetable stock
juice of 1 lemon

Remove 12 leaves from the outside of the head of Chinese leaves and plunge into a pan of boiling water. Leave for 1 minute, then drain and place the leaves in a bowl of cold water.

In another bowl, mix together the rice, tomatoes, nuts, herbs and salt and pepper to taste. Place a tablespoon of the filling on each of the blanched Chinese leaves and roll them up neatly, taking care not to tear them.

Shred the remaining Chinese leaves and place in the bottom of a large shallow pan. Arrange the cabbage parcels on top and pour in the stock and lemon juice. Bring the liquid to the boil. Reduce the heat and simmer, covered, for 30 minutes or until the cabbage parcels are cooked through and tender.

Stuffed Aubergines

Toast the bulgar under the grill before using in this recipe.

1 large onion, finely chopped
1 tablespoon cooking oil
50 g/2 oz bulgar or cracked
  wheat, toasted
150 ml/¼ pint vegetable stock
4 small or 2 large aubergines
4 tablespoons freshly chopped
  parsley

1 tablespoon freshly chopped
  mint
50 g/2 oz pine nuts, roughly
  chopped
¼ teaspoon ground coriander
150 ml/¼ pint tomato juice
salt and pepper

Fry the onion in the cooking oil until lightly browned. Stir in the bulgar, then pour on the stock. Bring to the boil. Reduce the heat and simmer for 30 minutes or until the bulgar is cooked and all the liquid has been absorbed.

Cut the aubergines in half and scoop out a small amount of flesh from the centre of each half. Dice the scooped-out flesh very finely and mix with the cooked bulgar. Stir in the parsley, mint, pine nuts and coriander and bind with a few tablespoons of tomato juice. Add salt and pepper to taste. Use this mixture to stuff the aubergine halves.

Place the stuffed aubergines in a shallow ovenproof dish. Pour the remaining tomato juice round the aubergines. Cover with foil and bake at 190°C/375°F/Gas 5 for 35–40 minutes.

Chestnut and Cabbage Casserole

This recipe is also very good made with red cabbage or with a mixture of green and white cabbage. Finish in cream, soured cream or soya milk according to taste.

1 large onion, sliced
450 g/1 lb white cabbage, shredded
1 carrot, grated
125 ml/4 fl oz vegetable stock
2 tablespoons white wine
pinch mixed dried herbs
salt and pepper
175 g/6 oz cooked chestnuts, sliced
2 teaspoons cornflour
3–4 tablespoons cream, soured cream or soya milk

Mix the onion, cabbage and carrot together and press into a saucepan. Combine the stock, wine, herbs and salt and pepper to taste and pour over the vegetables. Cover very tightly and bring to the boil. Reduce the heat and cook very gently for about 1 hour or until the vegetables are tender.

Stir and add the chestnuts. Dissolve the cornflour in a little of the liquid from the pan. Stir this mixture into the vegetable mixture and simmer, stirring, for 2–3 minutes or until thickened. Add the cream, soured cream or soya milk and reheat without boiling, stirring well.

Vegetable Casserole with Walnut Topping

1 onion, finely chopped
1 tablespoon cooking oil
50 g/2 oz mushrooms, sliced
3 carrots, diced
4 sticks celery, chopped
1 head fennel, sliced

2 potatoes, diced
1 × 400 g/14 oz can tomatoes,
  coarsely chopped
½ teaspoon mixed dried herbs
salt and pepper

Topping
100 g/4 oz wholemeal flour
pinch salt
50 g/2 oz butter or firm
  margarine

75 g/3 oz walnuts, finely
  chopped

Fry the onion in the cooking oil for about 3 minutes or until it turns translucent. Add the remaining vegetables except the tomatoes and fry gently for a further 2–3 minutes. Transfer to a casserole dish and pour on the tomatoes mixed with the herbs and salt and pepper to taste.

To make the topping, place the flour and salt in a bowl and add the butter or margarine cut into small pieces. Rub the fat into the flour until the mixture resembles fine breadcrumbs. Stir in the walnuts. Sprinkle the mixture all over the top of the vegetables.

Bake at 180°C/350°F/Gas 4 for about 1 hour or until the vegetables are cooked through and the topping is brown and crisp.

Mushroom, Cheese and Oatmeal Savoury

225 g/8 oz button mushrooms,
  sliced
3 tablespoons cooking oil
½ teaspoon garlic salt
¼ teaspoon dried thyme
freshly ground black pepper
1 large onion, finely chopped
75 g/3 oz oatmeal

150 ml/¼ pint vegetable stock or
  water
1 teaspoon miso, or ¼ teaspoon
  yeast extract
salt
1 egg, beaten
100 g/4 oz cheese, grated

Fry the mushrooms gently in 2 tablespoons of the oil for about 5 minutes or until tender. Stir from time to time. Stir in the garlic salt, thyme and pepper to taste and spoon into a shallow entrée or flan dish.

Fry the onion in the remaining oil for 5 minutes or until it turns translucent. Add the oatmeal and stir well, then add the stock, miso or yeast extract and salt to taste. Continue cooking over a low heat, stirring frequently, until the mixture thickens. This will take about 10 minutes.

Remove from the heat and beat in the egg and the cheese. Spoon the mixture over the mushrooms and bake at 200°C/400°F/Gas 6 for about 45 minutes or until set.

Cheese and Barley Soufflé

100 g/4 oz flaked barley
600 ml/1 pint milk or soya milk
1 teaspoon salt
75 g/3 oz farmhouse Cheddar
  cheese, grated

50 g/2 oz fresh Parmesan cheese,
  grated
4 eggs, separated

Cook the barley flakes in the milk (in a heavy pan or in a double saucepan) for 45 minutes or until the mixture is thick. Add the salt. Leave to cool a little, then purée in a blender or food processor. Stir in the cheeses and egg yolks.

Whisk the egg whites until they are very stiff. Stir a table-spoonful into the cereal mixture, then fold in the rest. Spoon into a greased 20 cm/8 in soufflé dish and bake at 200°C/400°F/Gas 6 for 35 minutes.

Boston Baked Cereals

This variation on Boston Baked Beans makes a hearty meal if served with a large green salad and crusty bread.

1 onion, chopped
1 tablespoon cooking oil
100 g/4 oz whole wheat berries, soaked overnight in cold water and drained
100 g/4 oz pot barley, washed and drained
100 g/4 oz dried haricot beans, soaked overnight in cold water and drained

1 × 400 g/14 oz can tomatoes
1 tablespoon soya flour
2 tablespoons molasses or black treacle
1 tablespoon tomato ketchup
1 teaspoon made mustard
salt and pepper
75 ml/3 fl oz water

Gently fry the onion in the cooking oil until it turns translucent. Mix with all the remaining ingredients and transfer to an earthenware casserole. Cover and bake at 180°C/350°F/Gas 4 for 1–1½ hours or until the beans and cereals are tender and most of the liquid has been absorbed.

Sweetcorn and Barley Risotto

1 tablespoon cooking oil
1 large onion, finely chopped
1 green pepper, seeded and finely chopped
1 carrot, diced
100 g/4 oz wholegrain or pot barley, washed and drained
salt and pepper

½ teaspoon yeast extract
450 ml/¾ pint boiling water
200 g/7 oz sweetcorn kernels, frozen or canned
50 g/2 oz Edam cheese, grated (optional)
1 tablespoon freshly chopped parsley

Heat the cooking oil in a saucepan and fry the onion for 2–3 minutes. Add the green pepper and carrot and continue frying gently for a further 3–4 minutes, taking care not to brown the vegetables. Next add the barley and salt and pepper to taste and stir well. Dissolve the yeast extract in the boiling water and pour over the barley and vegetables. Bring to the boil, then turn down the heat to the lowest it will go and cover with a lid. Simmer very gently for 20 minutes. Add the sweetcorn, stir once and continue cooking until all the liquid has been absorbed and the barley is tender. Serve sprinkled with cheese if using and chopped parsley.

Chestnut Patties with Mushroom Sauce

To toast the sesame seeds place in the grill pan and place under a hot grill. Stir frequently until brown. Leave to cool, then grind in a blender or food processor.

1 onion, finely chopped
1 carrot, grated
50 g/2 oz mushrooms, finely chopped
1 stick celery, finely chopped
50 g/2 oz cooked or canned chestnuts, puréed
½ tablespoon tomato purée
50 g/2 oz fresh wholemeal breadcrumbs

2 tablespoons maizemeal or soya flour
25 g/1 oz ground toasted sesame seeds
4 tablespoons freshly chopped parsley
½ teaspoon celery salt
2 eggs, beaten
cooking oil
flaked millet

Sauce

25 g/1 oz butter or firm margarine
100 g/4 oz mushrooms, finely chopped
1 tablespoon wholemeal flour

1 tablespoon maizemeal or flour
450 ml/¾ pint milk
salt and pepper

Mix together the onion, carrot, mushrooms, celery, chestnuts, tomato purée, breadcrumbs, maizemeal, sesame seeds, parsley and celery salt in a bowl. Add one egg or just sufficient to form a stiffish dough. Shape the mixture into 8 patties or cakes. Dip in the remaining egg, then coat in millet flakes. Heat the oil in a frying pan and gently fry the patties over a very low heat for about 15 minutes on each side or until golden in colour.

Meanwhile, heat the butter or margarine in another pan and fry the mushrooms for 5–6 minutes. Stir in the flour and maizemeal and the milk and bring to the boil, stirring all the time. Season to taste with salt and pepper and cook for 2–3 minutes. Serve with the patties.

Hazelnut Loaf with Fennel Sauce

Loaf

2 onions, very finely chopped
½ green pepper, seeded and
   finely chopped
3 sticks celery, very finely
   chopped
1 carrot, finely grated
100 g/4 oz fresh wholemeal
   breadcrumbs

75 g/3 oz hazelnuts, ground
2 eggs
1 tablespoon tomato purée
½ teaspoon ground cumin
1 teaspoon dried mixed herbs
salt and pepper
2 tablespoons flaked millet

Sauce

2 heads fennel, cut into
   segments
2 tablespoons cornflour

150 ml/¼ pint double cream
salt and pepper

Mix together all the loaf ingredients, except the flaked millet, in a bowl and shape into a loaf. Coat with flaked millet and place on a baking tray. Bake at 180°C/350°F/Gas 4 for about 1¼–1½ hours or until crisp on the outside and cooked through in the middle.

Meanwhile, cook the fennel in a steamer or in a very little water for 15–20 minutes or until tender. Drain well, retaining the liquid, and purée in a blender or food processor, or rub through a sieve. Mix with the cornflour and cream and bring to the boil. Gradually stir in sufficient fennel cooking liquid to give a thick creamy sauce. Season to taste with salt and pepper. Serve with the hazelnut loaf.

Lentil Peanut Loaf

Serve with Tomato Sauce (see page 28) or Mushroom Sauce (see page 56).

225 g/8 oz split lentils	1½ teaspoons yeast extract
1 medium onion, chopped	125 g/4 oz unsalted peanuts,
1 large carrot, grated	roughly chopped
750 ml/1¼ pints vegetable stock,	50 g/2 oz fresh wholewheat
made with 2 vegetable stock	breadcrumbs
cubes	2 eggs
1 teaspoon dried thyme	salt and pepper

Place the lentils, onion, carrot, stock and thyme in a saucepan. Bring to the boil and skim. Simmer for 20–25 minutes or until the lentils are tender, stirring occasionally. Mix in the yeast extract, peanuts, breadcrumbs and eggs. Add salt and pepper to taste.

Turn the mixture into a greased 1 kg/2 lb loaf tin. Bake at 180°C/350°F/Gas 4 for 1–1¼ hours or until firm in the centre. Leave to stand for 10 minutes before serving.

Oat and Rye Pizzas

You can use either oats or rye in this delicious pizza base. However, the oatmeal may need to be ground to a finer flour.

175 g/6 oz wholemeal flour	½ packet micronised dried yeast
50 g/2 oz very fine oatmeal or	175–200 ml/6–6½ fl oz
rye flour	lukewarm water
1 teaspoon salt	

Topping
cooking oil	
4 tablespoons tomato purée	3 tomatoes, peeled and sliced
100 g/4 oz Cheddar cheese,	sliced stuffed olives
grated	
75 g/3 oz mushrooms, sliced	

Place the wholemeal flour, oatmeal or rye flour, salt and yeast in a bowl. Pour on the water and mix to a soft dough. Place in a greased bowl and cover with a cloth. Leave to rise in a warm place for about 1 hour or until doubled in size.

Knock down and roll out with a rolling pin. Use to line round pizza pans or a large 28 × 18 cm/11 × 7 in rectangular tray. Brush with cooking oil, then spread with the tomato purée. Next cover with cheese, mushrooms and tomato slices. Dot with olives to taste and bake at 220°C/425°F/Gas 7 for 20 minutes or until the pizza is cooked through.

Stuffed Buckwheat Pancakes

Pancakes

1½ teaspoons dried yeast
450 ml/¾ pint warm water
175 g/6 oz buckwheat flour

1 teaspoon salt
2 small eggs, beaten
cooking oil

Filling

450 g/1 lb frozen chopped
    spinach, thawed
butter
300 g/10 oz quark
2 tablespoons flaked brazil nuts
    or almonds

1 tablespoon raisins
½ teaspoon ground coriander
salt and pepper

Mix the dried yeast with a little of the warm water and leave to stand in a warm place until it begins to froth. Add the rest of the water, the buckwheat flour and salt and beat well with a wire whisk to remove any lumps. Leave to stand for 10 minutes.

Meanwhile, heat the spinach in a knob of butter. Add the quark and mix well together. Add the remaining filling ingredients and heat through.

Beat the eggs into the buckwheat mixture. Heat a non-stick

pancake or frying pan and grease with a very little oil. Drop 3 tablespoons of the batter into the pan and tilt the pan to spread it out evenly. Cook until the bottom of the pancake starts to brown. Turn over and cook the other side. Remove the pancake and keep hot. Repeat this process until all the buckwheat mixture has been used up.

Spoon a little of the spinach mixture into the centre of each pancake. Roll up and place on a serving dish. Serve at once or quickly heat through in a hot oven.

Tacos with Kasha Beans and Chilli Sauce

2 tablespoons cooking oil
1 × 425 g/15 oz can red kidney
  beans, drained
1 sachet chilli sauce
1 sachet taco seasoning mix
100 ml/4 fl oz water
50 g/2 oz toasted buckwheat
25 g/1 oz butter
1 packet taco shells
2 tomatoes, cut into wedges
50 g/2 oz Cheddar cheese, grated
8 lettuce leaves, shredded

Heat the cooking oil in a saucepan and add the beans, taco seasoning, chilli sauce and water. Bring to the boil, stirring well. Place the toasted buckwheat and butter in a casserole dish and pour the bean and chilli mixture over the top. Bake at 190°C/375°F/Gas 5 for 5 minutes or until the buckwheat is light and fluffy and most of the liquid has been absorbed.

Meanwhile, heat the taco shells in the oven as directed on the packet. Spoon a little of the kasha and bean mixture into each shell. Top with tomatoes, cheese and lettuce.

Cheese and Walnut Picnic Loaf

Use different types of cheese to give a variety of flavours to this cold dish.

225 g/8 oz Cheshire cheese,
  grated
1 carrot, grated
50 g/2 oz walnuts, very finely
  chopped
6 small cocktail gherkins, finely
  chopped

1 teaspoon French mustard
salt and pepper
1 tablespoon mayonnaise
1 tablespoon soured cream

Mix all the ingredients in a bowl and press into a non-stick loaf tin. Chill for 2 hours. Turn out and slice carefully to serve.

Peanut Wheat Roll

175 g/6 oz curd cheese
50 g/2 oz salted or unsalted
  peanuts, finely chopped
25 g/1 oz sprouted wheat

2 hard-boiled eggs, chopped
4 spring onions, very finely
  chopped
salt and pepper

Beat the curd cheese with a wooden spoon until smooth, then stir in all the other ingredients to form a stiff mixture. Thin with a little milk if too stiff. Shape into a sausage and wrap in foil or cling film. Chill for at least 1 hour. Cut into slices to serve with salad or in open sandwiches.

Stuffed Chicory Spears

Add other fresh herbs from the garden in season. I particularly like lemon balm or chervil.

75 g/3 oz whole wheat grains or berries, soaked in cold water overnight and drained
150 ml/¼ pint vegetable stock
6 spring onions, chopped
2 tablespoons freshly chopped parsley

100 g/4 oz cottage cheese
salt and pepper
2 heads chicory, opened out into spears
2 tablespoons flaked Brazil nuts

Cook the wheat in the vegetable stock for 1 hour. Drain and leave to get cold.

Mix the spring onions, parsley, cottage cheese and cold wheat berries together. Season to taste with salt and pepper and use to fill the 12 largest chicory spears. Sprinkle the top with Brazil flakes.

CHAPTER FIVE

Accompaniments

Sweet Potatoes with Coconut

4 medium-sized sweet potatoes
25 g/1 oz butter or margarine
1 small orange, peeled and
  chopped

1 tablespoon brown sugar
¼ teaspoon grated nutmeg
40 g/1½ oz desiccated coconut

Bake the sweet potatoes in their jackets at 190°C/375°F/Gas 5 for about 1 hour or until tender. Cut a slice from the top of each sweet potato. Remove most of the flesh from the sweet potato skins, keeping the skins intact. Mash the flesh with a fork and beat in the remaining ingredients except the coconut.

Return the mixture to the potato skins and sprinkle the tops with the coconut. Bake at 200°C/400°F/Gas 6 for 10 minutes or until the coconut is lightly browned.

Stir-fried Summer Vegetables with Toasted Cashews

75 g/3 oz cashew nuts
cooking oil
1 clove garlic, finely chopped
225 g/8 oz mange-tout peas,
  topped and tailed
100 g/4 oz very small French
  beans, topped and tailed

225 g/8 oz new carrots, thinly
  sliced
100 g/4 oz courgettes, thinly
  sliced
50 ml/2 fl oz vegetable stock
1 tablespoon soy sauce
2 tablespoons dry sherry

Heat a frying pan over a moderate heat and dry fry the cashew nuts for about 3 minutes to brown them lightly. Set them aside. Brush the frying pan with oil and stir-fry the garlic for 30 seconds. Add the peas, beans and carrots and stir-fry for 1 minute. Add the courgettes and continue stirring for 2 minutes. Pour on the stock, soy sauce and sherry and bring quickly to the boil, stirring. Simmer for 1–2 minutes or until the vegetables are just tender. Serve at once, sprinkled with the cashew nuts. Serves 6.

Succotash

Lima beans can usually be bought in cans; however, the French flageolet can also be used in this recipe and these are available canned or dried. Soak dried beans overnight in cold water before cooking in plenty of boiling water for about 1 hour.

½ small onion, finely chopped
1 tablespoon cooking oil
1 dessertspoon plain flour
150 ml/¼ pint single cream or
  soya milk
1 × 450 g/1 lb can lima or
  flageolet beans, well drained

200 g/7 oz sweetcorn kernels,
  canned or frozen
salt and pepper
pinch dried savory

Fry the onion in the cooking oil until lightly browned. Stir in the flour and then the cream or soya milk. Bring to the boil. Add all the remaining ingredients and return to the boil. Simmer for 5 minutes and serve.

Barley Mushroom Bake

1 large onion, finely chopped
2 tablespoons cooking oil
1 carrot, grated
225 g/8 oz mushrooms, sliced

175 g/6 oz pot barley, washed
  and drained
250 ml/8 fl oz vegetable stock
½ teaspoon dried marjoram
salt and pepper

Gently fry the onion in the cooking oil until it turns translucent. Add the carrot and mushrooms. Continue cooking for 3–4 minutes or until the vegetables begin to soften. Add the barley and stir to make sure it is well coated with fat. Transfer the mixture to a casserole dish and pour on the stock. Add the herbs and salt and pepper to taste. Stir and cover. Bake at 180°C/350°F/Gas 4 for 1 hour or until the barley is tender.

Orange and Almond Barley Pilaff

25 g/1 oz blanched almonds,
  halved
5 cardamom pods
100 g/4 oz pot barley, washed
  and drained
600 ml/1 pint vegetable stock
½ teaspoon ground turmeric

pinch ground ginger
strip thinly-pared orange rind
juice of 1 orange
salt and pepper

Heat a frying pan over a moderate heat and dry fry the almonds for 5 minutes, shaking the pan frequently. Set them aside. Split the cardamom pods and release the seeds. Toast the seeds in the frying pan over moderate heat for about

5 minutes, stirring frequently. Remove the **seeds** and crush them in a grinder or pestle and mortar.

Put the barley into the frying pan with the crushed cardamom seeds, the stock, turmeric, ginger, orange rind and juice. Season to taste with salt and pepper. Bring to the boil, stir well and cover. Simmer over a low heat for about 1½ hours or until the barley is tender and the stock has been absorbed. If there is any remaining liquid, turn up the heat and boil it off. Remove and discard the orange rind. Turn onto a heated dish and scatter with the toasted almonds.

Coconut Wheat

Whole oats and barley can be treated in the same way as the wheat berries in this recipe.

½ fresh coconut, grated
300 ml/½ pint boiling water
75 g/3 oz wheat berries
75 g/3 oz cracked wheat or bulgar
salt and pepper

Place the fresh coconut in a bowl and pour on the boiling water. Leave to cool. Pour off the liquid and soak the wheat berries in it overnight. Dry the coconut on kitchen paper and toast under the grill. Keep on one side.

The next day, bring the wheat berries and coconut milk to the boil and simmer for 30 minutes. Add the cracked wheat, stir and return to the boil. Continue cooking for a further 30 minutes or until all the liquid has been absorbed. Season to taste with salt and pepper. Add a little of the toasted coconut or serve with it sprinkled over the top. Keep the remainder of the coconut for other recipes.

Wheat Berries, Stewed with Tomatoes

100 g/4 oz whole wheat berries, soaked overnight in cold water
1 × 400 g/14 oz can tomatoes
300 ml/½ pint vegetable stock
½ teaspoon mixed dried herbs
salt and pepper

Drain the wheat berries and place in a saucepan with all the remaining ingredients. Bring to the boil. Reduce the heat, cover and simmer for 1 hour until the wheat is tender.

Mixed Vegetables with Cracked Wheat

100 g/4 oz cracked wheat or bulgar
75 ml/3 fl oz tomato juice
200 ml/7 fl oz water
salt and pepper
2 × 225 g/8 oz packets stir-fry mixed vegetables
butter

Place the cracked wheat, tomato juice, water and salt and pepper to taste in a saucepan and bring to the boil. Reduce the heat and simmer very gently for about 30 minutes or until the wheat is cooked and all the liquid has been absorbed.

Cook the stir-fry vegetables in butter as directed on the packet, and when tender mix with the cooked bulgar.

Bulgar Rice

Use a vegetable stock cube or yeast extract and water to vary the flavour of this dish. It can also be made with half tomato juice and half water.

175 g/6 oz brown rice
75 g/3 oz bulgar
600 ml/1 pint vegetable stock
salt

25 g/1 oz peanuts
25 g/1 oz butter, melted
1 tablespoon freshly chopped
    parsley or chives

Wash the rice and bulgar and drain. Bring the vegetable stock to the boil and add the rice, bulgar and salt to taste. Stir once, then cover and simmer for 40–45 minutes or until the rice is tender and all the liquid has been absorbed. Turn off the heat and leave to stand for a further 10 minutes before fluffing up with a fork. Transfer to a serving dish.

Fry the nuts in the butter until browned and pour over the rice. Sprinkle with parsley and serve.

Slikh

To speed up preparation of this recipe use canned flageolet in place of the dried flageolet or black eye beans. These do not need to be cooked and can be added with the spinach and bulgar.

50 g/2 oz dried flageolet or black
    eye beans, soaked overnight in
    cold water
450 ml/¾ pint water
225 g/8 oz frozen chopped
    spinach, thawed
50 g/2 oz bulgar

1 teaspoon freshly chopped
    parsley
1 teaspoon lemon juice
pinch grated nutmeg
salt and pepper

Drain the beans and place in a saucepan with 300 ml/½ pint of the water. Bring to the boil and simmer for 1 hour or until almost tender.

Stir in the spinach, bulgar and remaining water. Return to the boil and simmer for a further 20–30 minutes or until everything is cooked through. Stir in the lemon juice, nutmeg and salt and pepper to taste.

Sesame Bulgar with Peas

1 tablespoon cooking oil
25 g/1 oz sesame seeds
175 g/6 oz bulgar
75 g/3 oz frozen peas
salt and pepper
300 ml/½ pint vegetable stock made with ½ tsp yeast extract and
   water

Heat the oil in a wide saucepan and quickly fry the sesame seeds. Add the bulgar and stir until it is well coated with oil. Add the remaining ingredients, stir and bring to the boil. Cover tightly, reduce the heat and simmer for 15 minutes or until the bulgar has absorbed all the liquid.

Vegetable Couscous

Use wholemeal couscous for this recipe.

2 tablespoons cooking oil
seeds from 4 cardamom pods
6 black peppercorns
2 cloves
pinch fennel or celery seeds
1 onion, finely chopped
1 clove garlic, finely chopped
1 teaspoon grated fresh root
   ginger

1 large potato, diced
50 g/2 oz frozen peas
½ red pepper, seeded and diced
175 g/6 oz wholewheat couscous
350 ml/12 fl oz boiling water
salt and pepper
1 tablespoon freshly chopped
   coriander or parsley

Heat the cooking oil in a saucepan and fry the cardamom seeds, peppercorns, cloves and fennel or celery seeds for about 1 minute. Add the onion, garlic and root ginger and continue frying until lightly browned. Add the remaining vegetables and gently fry over a low heat for about 6–8 minutes, stirring from time to time. Next stir in the couscous and pour on the water. Cover the pan and bring to the boil. Simmer gently for 20 minutes or until the couscous is cooked and all the liquid has been absorbed. Add salt and pepper to taste and serve sprinkled with coriander or parsley.

Millet with Lentils or Split Peas

If using split peas soak for 2 hours in hot water. Serve with creamed spinach and a spicy onion and tomato salad to make a complete meal.

225 g/8 oz whole millet
2 tablespoons cooking oil
1 teaspoon cumin seeds
2 small onions, finely chopped
1 clove garlic, finely chopped
75 g/3 oz split lentils or soaked
   and drained split peas

1 teaspoon ground coriander
½ teaspoon ground turmeric
600 ml/1 pint vegetable stock
1 green chilli, seeded and cut
   into strips (optional)

Dry-fry the millet in a hot non-stick frying pan until well toasted all over. Remove from the pan and keep on one side. Heat half the cooking oil in the pan and fry the cumin seeds for 1 minute. Add one of the onions and the garlic and fry until lightly browned. Stir in the lentils or peas, the millet and the spices. Next add the stock and bring to the boil. Stir and cover with a lid. Reduce the heat and simmer very gently for 30 minutes.

Check to see if more liquid is required, then stir and continue cooking for 10–15 minutes or until the millet and lentils or peas are fully cooked. Remove from the heat and leave to stand with the lid on.

Heat the remaining oil until very hot and add the second onion and the chilli if using. Fry until well browned. Stir into the millet mixture and serve.

Aubergine Millet

2 tablespoons cooking oil
1 tablespoon sesame seeds
½ small onion
1 small aubergine, diced
225 g/8 oz whole millet

550 ml/14 fl oz vegetable stock or
    water
salt and pepper
2 tablespoons freshly chopped
    parsley

Heat the oil in a saucepan and fry the sesame seeds quickly until lightly browned. Add the onion and aubergine and brown all over for about 3–4 minutes. Stir in the millet and pour on the stock or water. Add salt and pepper to taste and 1 tablespoon parsley and bring to the boil. Reduce the heat, cover and cook very gently over a very low heat for about 35 minutes or until all the liquid has been absorbed and the millet is tender. Sprinkle with the remaining parsley and serve.

Baked Buckwheat Kasha

175 g/6 oz buckwheat kasha
50 g/2 oz butter
1 teaspoon salt
boiling water

Brown the kasha under the grill. Grease a heavy ovenproof dish. Put the kasha in this. Dot with the butter and sprinkle with salt. Pour on sufficient boiling water just to cover the kasha. Cover with greaseproof paper and a lid and place in a baking tin filled with 2 cm/1 in hot water. Bake at 190°C/375°F/ Gas 5 for 30 minutes or until cooked through.

Kasha Browns

This recipe can also be made with bulgar.

40 g/1½ oz toasted buckwheat or
  kasha
350 g/12 oz potatoes, diced
175 ml/6 fl oz boiling water
1 teaspoon salt
1 large onion, finely chopped

3 tablespoons cooking oil
1 small red or green pepper,
  seeded and diced
freshly ground black pepper

Place the buckwheat and potatoes in a saucepan and add the boiling water and salt. Return to the boil, then reduce the heat and simmer for about 35 minutes or until all the liquid has been absorbed and the kasha and potatoes are cooked through.

Fry the onion in 1 tablespoon of the cooking oil until lightly browned. Add the red or green pepper and continue cooking until the pepper is soft. Stir into the kasha and potatoes. Add pepper to taste.

Heat the remaining oil in a frying pan and fry spoonfuls of the mixture until crisp and brown on each side.

Tomato Polenta

450 g/1 lb tomatoes, peeled, chopped and puréed
25 g/1 oz butter
600 ml/1 pint vegetable stock
175 g/6 oz polenta or yellow cornmeal
1 teaspoon sugar
salt and pepper

Heat the tomatoes with the butter, stirring until the butter has melted. Add the vegetable stock and bring to the boil. Gradually add the polenta or cornmeal in a thin stream, stirring vigorously to prevent any lumps forming. Add the sugar and plenty of salt and pepper. Continue cooking over a gentle heat for 20–30 minutes, stirring frequently, until the polenta comes easily away from the sides of the pan.

Serve on a warmed serving plate with more butter, or leave to cool, covered with greaseproof paper or foil, and then cut into slices about 1 cm/½ in thick. Shallow fry the slices in plenty of cooking oil for about 3 minutes on each side until crisp. Drain on kitchen paper before serving.

CHAPTER SIX

Salads

Gingered Vegetable Salad with Cashew Nuts

50 g/2 oz cashew nuts, roughly
   chopped
1 × 225 g/8 oz can water
   chestnuts, drained and sliced
2 carrots, thinly sliced
75 g/3 oz frozen peas
2 sticks celery, thinly sliced

150 ml/¼ pint orange juice
2 tablespoons sherry
1 tablespoon soy sauce
1 teaspoon grated fresh root
   ginger
salt and pepper

Dry-fry the cashew nuts in a hot frying pan until they are well browned. Keep on one side. Place all the remaining ingredients in a saucepan and bring to the boil. Cover and simmer for about 10 minutes or until the carrots are almost tender. Leave to cool, then chill for 1 hour. Serve sprinkled with the toasted cashew nuts.

Mixed Bean Salad with Walnut Dressing

This dressing will keep in the fridge for a couple of weeks, so make up the full quantity and use as required.

1 × 425 g/15 oz can red kidney beans, drained and rinsed
100 g/4 oz cooked broad beans
100 g/4 oz cooked carrots, sliced

50 g/2 oz sprouted soya beans or lentils
shredded lettuce

Dressing
10 walnut halves, crushed
3 tablespoons light soy sauce
3 tablespoons cider vinegar

1 tablespoon dark brown sugar
freshly ground black pepper

Start by making up the dressing. Mix all the ingredients together in a jam jar, cover and store in the fridge for at least 24 hours before using.

Mix together all the salad ingredients except the lettuce. Arrange the lettuce in a serving dish. Spoon on the bean mixture, then pour 2 or 3 tablespoons of the dressing over the top.

Cucumber and Celery Salad with Toasted Cashews

This salad is very good served on a bed of grated carrot.

75 g/3 oz cashew nuts, roughly chopped
7–8 sticks celery, chopped
10 cm/4 in piece cucumber, diced
¼ green pepper, seeded and very finely chopped
2 small tomatoes, peeled, seeded and chopped

1 tablespoon raisins
4 tablespoons soured cream
1 teaspoon lemon juice
salt and pepper

Dry-fry the cashews in a hot non-stick frying pan until toasted. Leave on one side to cool. Toss the celery and cucumber in a bowl. Combine all the remaining ingredients and spoon over the celery and cucumber. Top with the toasted cashews.

Italian Raddichio Salad with Pine Nut Dressing

1 head raddichio
1 head chicory

a few lettuce leaves

Dressing
2 tablespoons pine nuts
6 tablespoons olive oil
3 tablespoons wine vinegar
pinch grated nutmeg

piece thinly-pared lemon rind
¼ teaspoon dried tarragon
salt and pepper

To make the dressing, spread the pine nuts on a baking tray and bake at 190°C/375°F/Gas 5 for 7–8 minutes or until they are golden brown in colour. Mix all the remaining dressing ingredients in a jam jar. Add the baked nuts, cover the jar and shake well together. Leave to stand for at least 24 hours before using.

Wash the salad leaves and place in the salad compartment of the fridge to crisp up a little. Tear all the salad leaves into 2 or 3 pieces and toss in 3–4 tablespoons of the dressing. Store any remaining dressing in the fridge for another day.

Fennel and Almond Salad

If you prefer a more crunchy salad, simply use the fennel raw. However, you will need to slice it finely, and slice the mushrooms. Vegans can substitute vinaigrette dressing for the mayonnaise.

2 small heads fennel, cut into
  quarters
50 g/2 oz flaked almonds
100 g/4 oz button mushrooms,
  cut into quarters
2 tablespoons mayonnaise

1 tablespoon lemon juice
1 tablespoon freshly chopped
  parsley
salt and pepper

Steam the fennel in a steamer or in a very little boiling water for about 5 minutes or until the vegetable is tender but still crisp. Drain and leave to cool.

Meanwhile, dry-fry the flaked almonds in a non-stick frying pan or toast under the grill. Cut the cold fennel into small chunks and mix with the mushrooms and two-thirds of the almonds. Mix together the mayonnaise, lemon juice, parsley and salt and pepper to taste and pour over the salad. Toss once or twice and serve sprinkled with the remaining toasted almonds.

Green Bean Salad with Peanut Dressing

This dressing can also be used on green leaf salads or to coat hard-boiled eggs.

350 g/12 oz French beans, topped and tailed
salt

Dressing
1 tablespoon peanut butter
juice and grated rind of 1 orange
milk

Steam the French beans in a steamer or in a very little boiling salted water for 5–6 minutes or until tender but still crisp. Drain and leave to cool.

Mix the peanut butter with the orange juice and rind and stir in sufficient milk to give a smooth creamy consistency. Arrange the beans on a serving plate and pour the dressing over the top.

Corn and Wholewheat Salad with Green Peppers

Toasted and coarsely chopped walnuts can be used to garnish this dish if walnut oil is used.

*100 g/4 oz cooked wholewheat
  berries*
*100 g/4 oz cooked sweetcorn
  kernels*
*1 green pepper, seeded and finely
  chopped*
*1 green chilli pepper, seeded and
  finely chopped*
*4 tomatoes, peeled, seeded and
  chopped*

2 tablespoons walnut or olive oil
2 teaspoons lime or lemon juice
a little grated lime or lemon rind
*freshly chopped parsley to
  garnish*

Mix all the ingredients in a large bowl and toss well together. Spoon onto a serving plate and sprinkle with parsley. Serve at once.

Potato Barley Salad with Soured Cream Dressing

*50 g/2 oz pot barley, washed and
  drained*
300 ml/½ pint vegetable stock
*450 g/1 lb potatoes, cut into
  chunks*
salt and pepper

*½ small onion or 6–7 spring
  onions, finely chopped*
*1 tablespoon freshly chopped
  parsley*
2 tablespoons lemon juice
4 tablespoons soured cream

Cook the pot barley in the vegetable stock for about 1 hour or until tender. Drain and leave to cool. Cook the potatoes in boiling salted water until tender. Drain and cut into smaller dice. Mix the potatoes with the onion, parsley and lemon juice while still hot. Leave to cool, then mix in the cooked barley and soured cream. Season to taste with salt and pepper and chill for 30 minutes before serving.

Bulgar Mountain with Bean Salad

*75 g/3 oz bulgar or cracked
  wheat
175 ml/6 fl oz water
2 hard-boiled eggs, chopped
3 spring onions, finely chopped
50 g/2 oz cooked peas
25 g/1 oz cooked sweetcorn
  kernels
¼ teaspoon dried tarragon
salt and pepper*

*2 tablespoons mayonnaise
1 × 400 g/14 oz can haricot
  beans, drained and rinsed
¼ green pepper, seeded and
  finely chopped
2 tablespoons freshly chopped
  parsley
1 tablespoon olive or nut oil
1 teaspoon lemon juice
watercress sprigs*

Soak the bulgar in the cold water for 1 hour. Squeeze out all the
excess water and mix the bulgar with the eggs, spring onions,
peas, sweetcorn and tarragon. Add salt and pepper to taste
and bind with the mayonnaise. Press into a greased pudding
basin and chill for 1 hour.

Meanwhile, toss the beans with the remaining ingredients,
except the watercress, and keep in the fridge until required. To
serve, turn out the bulgar mountain and surround with the
bean salad and sprigs of watercress.

Savoury Rice

*175 g/6 oz brown rice
600 ml/1 pint boiling water
100 g/4 oz frozen peas
50 g/2 oz pine nuts
25 g/1 oz flaked almonds
1 tablespoon raisins
4 spring onions, very finely
  chopped*

*¼ green pepper, seeded and
  finely chopped
2 tablespoons freshly chopped
  parsley
freshly ground black pepper
1 tablespoon cooking oil
1 tablespoon orange juice*

Cook the rice in the boiling water until all the liquid has been
absorbed and the rice is tender. Rinse well to remove all the

starch and leave to drain and cool. Cook the peas as directed on the packet. Drain and leave to cool.

Mix the rice and peas with all the remaining ingredients. Chill for 30 minutes before serving.

Coconut Chutney

If you cannot get fresh coriander for this recipe use ½ teaspoon ground coriander with ¼ teaspoon ground cumin.

½ fresh coconut, chopped
1 green chilli, seeded and chopped
1 tablespoon chopped fresh coriander
¼ teaspoon salt
juice of 2 lemons or limes

Place the coconut, chilli, coriander and salt in a food processor and process until well chopped. Add sufficient lemon or lime juice to give a thick batter-like consistency. Place in the fridge to chill and thicken a little.

Serve with lentil dishes and curry

CHAPTER SEVEN

Desserts

Date and Hazelnut Fruit Crumble

Use any kind of fruit in season for the base.

1 kg/2 lb cooking apples, peeled, cored and sliced
a little grated lemon rind
honey or sugar to sweeten
50 g/2 oz wholemeal flour
25 g/1 oz medium-fine oatmeal

25 g/1 oz hazelnuts, finely chopped
50 g/2 oz butter or firm margarine
50 g/2 oz light muscovado sugar

Rinse the slices of cooking apple in water. Drain well and place in a saucepan with the lemon rind. Cook over a low heat until the apples are tender. Mash well and stir in honey or sugar to taste. Spoon into a pie dish. Mix together the flour, oatmeal and nuts and add the fat, cut into small pieces. Rub into the dry ingredients until the mixture resembles fine breadcrumbs. Stir in the sugar and spoon over the top of the apples. Bake at 180°C/350°F/Gas 4 for 30–35 minutes.

Cashew and Date Sponge

750 g/1½ lb cooking apples, peeled, cored and sliced
225 g/8 oz cashew nuts
100 g/4 oz dates
50 g/2 oz sugar
3 eggs, separated
3½ tablespoons milk

Cook the apples with a very little water in a saucepan until almost tender. Transfer to a deep soufflé or pie dish.

Grind the nuts and dates in a food processor until the mixture reaches a stiff batter consistency. This takes quite a long time. Add the sugar and egg yolks and blend until well incorporated. Add the milk a little at a time to reach a soft dropping consistency. Whisk the egg whites separately to stiff peaks and fold into the date and nut mixture.

Spoon onto the apples and bake at 200°C/400°F/Gas 6 for 35 minutes or until cooked through.

Nut Pancakes with Lemon Sauce

Choose either ground almonds, hazelnuts or Brazils for this recipe – each will give you a different dish.

25 g/1 oz finely chopped nuts　　*2 eggs, beaten*
100 g/4 oz wholemeal flour,　　*300 ml/½ pint milk*
　sifted　　　　　　　　　　*cooking oil*
50 g/2 oz sugar
pinch salt

Sauce
juice of 2 lemons　　　　　*25 g/1 oz butter*
1 teaspoon honey

Spread out the nuts on a heatproof plate and toast under the grill. Keep turning the nuts with a spoon as they brown. Leave to cool, then mix with the flour, sugar and salt. Make a well in the centre and work in the eggs and then the milk. Leave the batter to stand for 30 minutes.

Heat a non-stick frying pan and brush with a very little oil. Pour about 3 tablespoons of the batter into the pan, tilting the pan to spread it evenly. Cook until the pancake is lightly browned underneath. Turn over and cook the other side. Remove the pancake and keep hot. Repeat the process until all the batter has been used up. Arrange the pancakes on a plate and keep warm.

Boil the lemon juice in a small saucepan until it is reduced to about 3 tablespoons. Stir in the honey, then beat in the butter a little at a time, using a wire whisk. When the sauce thickens a little, pour it over the pancakes.

Barley Apricot Soufflé

For a hot soufflé omit the Gelozone and add the orange juice to the barley mixture with the egg yolks. Spoon the mixture into a greased soufflé dish. Bake at 190°C/375°F/Gas 5 for 45–50 minutes or until set in the centre and serve immediately.

50 g/2 oz flaked barley
250 ml/8 fl oz milk
1 tablespoon light muscovado sugar
75 g/3 oz dried apricots, soaked overnight in cold water, drained and chopped

2 eggs, separated
15 g/½ oz Gelozone
juice of 1 orange

Place the barley, milk, sugar and apricots in the top of a double saucepan. Fill the bottom pan with water and bring to the boil. Cover the barley mixture with a lid and cook for about 10 minutes or until the barley and apricots are tender. Do not worry if the mixture curdles. When it is cooked purée in a blender or food processor, or rub through a sieve. Beat in the egg yolks.

Dissolve the Gelozone in the orange juice by placing in a pan and heating. Stir until the Gelozone mixture is clear and boil for one minute. Stir into the barley apricot purée.

Whisk the egg whites until very stiff. Stir a tablespoonful into the barley mixture, then carefully fold in the rest of the whites. Spoon into a glass dish. Chill until set.

Apple Pie with Nut Pastry

Almost any kind of ground nuts can be used in this pastry.

50 g/2 oz butter or firm
  margarine
100 g/4 oz wholemeal flour
50 g/2 oz ground walnuts

25 g/1 oz light muscovado sugar
1 egg, beaten

Filling
750 g/1½ lb cooking apples,
  peeled, cooked and puréed
2–3 eating apples, peeled, cored
  and sliced

3 tablespoons apricot jam

Rub the fat into the flour until the mixture resembles fine breadcrumbs. Stir in the walnuts and sugar and bind with sufficient beaten egg to give a firm dough. Roll or press out to line a 20 cm/8 in loose-bottomed flan tin.

Brush the pastry with any remaining egg and spoon in the puréed cooking apples. Arrange the slices of eating apples in concentric rings on the top. Heat the jam in a small pan and brush all over the top of the apple slices. Bake at 200°C/400°F/Gas 6 for about 40 minutes or until well browned on top.

Millet and Gooseberry Flan

Blackcurrants can be used in place of gooseberries.

8 wholewheat digestive biscuits,
    crushed
40 g/2 oz butter or firm
    margarine, melted
75 g/3 oz flaked millet
1 tablespoon honey

550 ml/14 fl oz milk
2 eggs, separated
1 × 220 g/7½ oz can
    gooseberries
15 g/½ oz Gelozone

Mix the digestive biscuits with the butter or margarine and press onto the bottom of an 18 cm/7 in loose-bottomed cake tin. Place in the refrigerator to chill.

Stir the millet, honey and milk together in the top of a double saucepan. Fill the bottom pan with water and bring to the boil. Cook the millet for 30 minutes or until the mixture is thick and creamy. Remove from the heat and leave to cool, then stir in the egg yolks.

Mix some of the juice from the can of gooseberries with the Gelozone and place in a small saucepan. Stir until the Gelozone dissolves. Add to the millet mixture. Purée the gooseberries and remaining juice in a blender or food processor, or rub through a sieve. Stir into the millet mixture. Whisk the egg whites until very stiff and fold into the gooseberry millet mixture.

Spoon onto the biscuit base and chill until set. Push out of the cake tin to serve.

Pear and Almond Pie

Pastry

75 g/3 oz wholemeal flour
50 g/2 oz fine maizemeal
25 g/1 oz medium cornmeal or
  polenta
100 g/4 oz firm margarine, cut
  into small pieces

75 g/3 oz golden granulated
  sugar
1 egg, beaten

Filling

4 ripe pears, peeled and sliced
2 tablespoons lemon juice
100 g/4 oz curd cheese
50 g/2 oz demerara sugar

a little grated lemon rind
75 g/3 oz ground almonds
¼ teaspoon almond essence

Sift the wholemeal flour and discard the bran. Stir in the maizemeal and cornmeal or polenta. Rub the fat into the dry ingredients until the mixture resembles fine breadcrumbs. Stir in the granulated sugar. Use sufficient egg to bind the mixture to a dough. Press out to line a 20 cm/8 in loose-bottomed flan tin.

Dip the sliced pears in lemon juice and arrange them on the bottom of the pastry case. Beat the curd cheese with the demerara sugar and lemon juice from the pears, then beat in the lemon rind, ground almonds and almond essence. Spread the mixture over the pears. Bake at 200°C/400°F/Gas 6 for 35 minutes. You may need to cover with foil after 20 minutes.

Wholewheat Pecan Pie

If you cannot get pecans, walnuts can be substituted but they are not as good for they are rather stronger in flavour and a little more oily.

Pastry
225 g/8 oz wholewheat flour
pinch of salt
100 g/4 oz firm margarine,
  softened

25 g/1 oz brown sugar
100 ml/4 fl oz cold water

Filling
175 g/6 oz butter
225 g/8 oz muscovado sugar
3 eggs
grated rind of two large lemons

juice of 1 large lemon
225 g/8 oz pecan nuts
whipped cream to decorate

Put the flour and salt into a bowl. Rub in the fat until the mixture resembles fine breadcrumbs. Stir in the sugar and then enough water to make a soft dough. Chill for 5 minutes, then roll out and use to line a 25 cm/10 in shallow flan tin. Bake blind at 180°C/350°F/Gas 4 for 10 minutes.

Meanwhile, cream the butter and sugar for the filling. Beat in the eggs one at a time. Add the lemon rind and juice and nuts. Mix well. Spoon into the pastry case. Return to the oven and continue baking at the same temperature for 45 minutes or until the filling is lightly browned. Remove from the oven and leave to cool. Serve with whipped cream.

Almond Meringues

3 egg whites
pinch cream of tartar
175 g/6 oz light muscovado
  sugar

25 g/1 oz flaked almonds

Filling
100 g/4 oz dried peaches, soaked
  overnight in cold water
25 g/1 oz ground almonds

150 ml/¼ pint double cream,
  whipped

To make the meringues, whisk the egg whites with the cream
of tartar until foamy, then gradually whisk in the sugar.
Continue whisking until the mixture is stiff and will not fall
out of the bowl when it is turned upside down. Fold in the
almonds. Place spoonfuls of the mixture on baking trays lined
with rice or parchment paper or make 2 large rounds of
meringue. Bake at 130°C/280°F/Gas ½ for about 1½ hours.
Leave the meringues to cool on a wire rack.

To make the filling, drain the peaches and cook with a very
little fresh water for about 30 minutes or until tender. Purée in
a blender or food processor, or rub through a sieve. Mix with
the ground almonds and fold in the cream. Use this mixture to
sandwich pairs of small meringues together or the 2 large
meringue rounds.

Nut and Ginger Yogurt

Use as a sauce for hot or cold puddings or eat on its own with
slices of raw apple.

1 teaspoon grated fresh root
  ginger
a little grated lemon or orange
  rind
25 g/1 oz hazelnuts or walnuts,
  coarsely chopped

25 g/1 oz cashew nuts or pine
  nuts, coarsely chopped
225 g/8 oz plain yogurt
sugar or honey to sweeten

Mix all the ingredients in a bowl and leave to stand in the fridge for about 1 hour before serving. If you do not like too strong a flavour of ginger use ½ teaspoon and chill for 30 minutes only.

Stuffed Apples

75 g/3 oz carob block
1 heaped dessertspoon peanut
  butter
1 teaspoon firm honey

40 g/1½ oz peanuts or other
  nuts, chopped
4 fresh green apples
1 teaspoon lemon juice

Break the carob block into a pudding basin and place in a saucepan of gently simmering water. When the carob has melted, stir in the peanut butter, honey and peanuts.

Core the apples and use the carob mixture to stuff the hole. Chill for 1 hour. To serve, slice the apples into rings and sprinkle with a very little lemon juice.

Apricot Almond Profiteroles   Makes 12

These profiteroles are crispier than those made with white flour but equally delicious.

150 ml/¼ pint water
50 g/2 oz butter
60 g/2½ oz wholemeal flour,
  weighed after most of the bran
  has been sifted out

pinch salt
1 egg

Filling

100 g/4 oz dried apricots, soaked
  for 2 hours in boiling water
40 g/1½ oz ground almonds

2 teaspoons brown sugar
150 ml/¼ pint double cream,
  whipped, or quark

Heat the water and butter in a saucepan. When the mixture boils, add the flour and salt and stir until the mixture comes away from the sides of the pan. Remove from the heat and beat in the egg. Place small spoonfuls of the mixture on a greased baking tray. Bake at 200°C/400°F/Gas 6 for 40–45 minutes or until the profiteroles are really crisp and dry. Leave to cool on a wire rack.

To make the filling, drain the apricots and place in a saucepan with a little fresh water. Bring to the boil and simmer for 20–30 minutes or until the fruit is tender. Drain, retaining 1 tablespoon of the liquid. Leave to cool. Purée the apricots in a blender or food processor with the reserved liquid or rub through a sieve and mix in the liquid. Stir in the ground almonds and sugar.

To make up the dessert, cut the profiteroles in half and fill the bases with the apricot almond purée. Add a little whipped cream or quark and replace the tops of the profiteroles.

Banana Cashew Creams

*100 g/4 oz cashew nut butter
    made without oil
    (see pages 29–30)*
50 g/2 oz dates
2 bananas
juice of ½ lemon

*3 tablespoons silken tofu or
    quark*
*1–2 tablespoons light muscovado
    sugar to taste*
*½ × 75 g/3 oz carob block,
    grated*

Add the dates to the cashew nut butter in the food processor and blend well together. Add the bananas, lemon juice, tofu or quark and sugar a little at a time. You should end up with a thick creamy consistency. Spoon into individual bowls and sprinkle the carob over the top. Chill and serve.

Hazelnut Icecream

*1 teaspoon cocoa or
    carob powder*
4 tablespoons milk
3 eggs

*3 tablespoons light muscovado
    sugar*
150 ml/¼ pint double cream
50 g/2 oz hazelnuts, chopped

Mix the cocoa or carob powder with a little of the milk. Heat the rest of the milk and stir into the cocoa. Leave to cool. Whisk the eggs with the sugar until thick and pale in colour. Whip the cold cocoa with the cream until it forms soft peaks. Fold in the hazelnuts, then fold the two mixtures together. Spoon into a container and freeze for 1 hour. Stir and freeze for a further 2 hours. Remove from the freezer 30 minutes before serving.

Greek Pastries

Phyllo pastry can be bought in specialist supermarkets and at Greek grocers. It is often available frozen.

50 g/2 oz hazelnuts, finely
   chopped
50 g/2 oz walnuts, finely
   chopped
50 g/2 oz pine nuts, finely
   chopped
50 g/2 oz raisins, finely chopped

50 g/2 oz lightly toasted fresh
   wholemeal breadcrumbs
6–8 tablespoons honey
6–8 sheets Greek phyllo pastry
25 g/1 oz butter, melted

Mix the nuts, raisins and breadcrumbs with the honey. Line the bottom of a greased 27 × 17 cm/7 × 11 in Swiss roll tin with 3–4 sheets of the pastry, brushing each layer with melted butter. Spread the nut and raisin mixture all over the pastry then top with a second layer of 3–4 pastry sheets, brushing each with butter. Bake at 180°C/350°F/Gas 4 for 35–40 minutes.

Cut into squares or fingers and serve with cream or yogurt.

CHAPTER EIGHT

Bread

Coconut Bread

For a less chewy bread grind the desiccated coconut in a blender before soaking in the milk.

75 g/3 oz desiccated coconut
150 ml/¼ pint milk
225 g/8 oz wholemeal flour
1 teaspoon baking powder
pinch salt

175 g/6 oz brown sugar
¼ teaspoon ground cinnamon
pinch ground allspice
25 g/1 oz butter or margarine,
* melted*

Mix the desiccated coconut and milk and leave to stand for 30 minutes. Sift the flour, baking powder and salt into a bowl and add the sugar and spices. Mix well together. Pour in the coconut and milk and beat in with a wooden spoon. Knead in the butter or margarine.

Spoon into a greased 450 g/1 lb loaf tin and bake at 180°C/350°F/Gas 4 for about 1¼ hours or until the loaf begins to come away from the sides of the tin. Leave to cool in the tin for 5 minutes, then turn out onto a wire rack.

Rye Baps   Makes 12

15 g/½ oz dried vitamin C yeast   *225 g/8 oz rye flour*
1 tablespoon dark muscovado   *350 g/12 oz wholemeal flour*
   sugar   *1 teaspoon salt*
450 ml/¾ pint lukewarm milk   *1 tablespoon vegetable oil*
2 tablespoons lukewarm water

Mix the yeast with the sugar and half the milk and leave to
stand in a warm place for 20 minutes. Stir in the rest of the milk
and the water. Place the flours and salt in a bowl and make a
well in the centre. Pour in the yeast and milk mixture and the
oil. Gradually draw the flour into the liquid and mix to form a
soft dough. Transfer to a floured surface and knead for 10
minutes or until the dough is smooth and elastic. Place in an
oiled bowl and cover with a clean cloth. Leave to rise in a warm
place for about 2 hours or until the dough has doubled in bulk.

   Knead again and divide the dough into 12 balls or rolls. Place
on a greased baking tray and leave in a warm place to rise
again. This will take about 30–40 minutes. Bake at 220°C/
425°F/Gas 7 for 20 minutes or until the rolls sound hollow
when tapped on the base.

Soda Bread with Oats

This bread should be eaten on the day it is made.

450 g/1 lb wholemeal flour,   *1 teaspoon cream of tartar*
   sifted   *300 ml/½ pint milk or soya milk*
100 g/4 oz fine oatmeal   *2 tablespoons treacle or cane*
1 teaspoon salt   *syrup*
1¼ teaspoons bicarbonate of
   soda

Place all the dry ingredients in a mixing bowl. Make a well in
the centre and add the milk and treacle or syrup. Mix well to

form a soft dough, adding a little more milk if necessary. Turn the dough out onto a floured board and knead for 1–2 minutes. Shape the dough into a round ball and place on a greased baking tray. Cut a deep cross on top of the loaf. Bake at 220°C/425°F/Gas 7 for 25–30 minutes or until the loaf is brown and sounds hollow when tapped on the base. Transfer to a wire rack and leave to cool a little. Eat warm or cold.

Wholemeal Bread with Cracked Wheat

350 g/12 oz wholemeal flour
100 g/4 oz cracked wheat
1 teaspoon salt
1 packet micronised dried yeast
400 ml/13 fl oz lukewarm water

Mix the flour, cracked wheat, salt and yeast in a bowl and gradually work in the water to form a soft dough. Transfer to a floured surface and knead for 8–10 minutes or until the dough is elastic. Transfer to a greased loaf tin or divide into 10–12 rolls and place on a greased baking tray. Leave in a warm place to rise for about 1 hour.

Bake the loaf at 200°C/400°F/Gas 6 for 35 minutes or the rolls at 230°C/450°F/Gas 8 for 10–12 minutes. Test loaf or rolls by tapping on the base: they should sound hollow.

Nut Bread

Almost any kind of nuts can be used in this recipe so experiment to see which flavours you like the best. Raisins can also be added for a change. In the Middle East spices such as cumin and fennel are also added.

2 teaspoons dried yeast
1 teaspoon light muscovado
   sugar
375 ml/13 fl oz lukewarm water
450 g/1 lb wholemeal flour

50 g/2 oz flaked almonds or
   Brazil nuts
25 g/1 oz walnuts, chopped
1 teaspoon salt

Mix the yeast, sugar and water in a measuring jug and leave to stand in a warm place for 20 minutes or until frothy. Place all the remaining ingredients in a bowl and make a well in the centre. Pour in the yeast liquid and mix by hand to form a soft dough. Transfer to a floured board and knead for 10 minutes. Shape into a loaf and place in a 450 g/1 lb loaf tin. Leave in a warm place to rise. This will take about 1 hour.

Bake at 200°C/400°F/Gas 6 for about 35 minutes or until the loaf sounds hollow when tapped on the base.

Oatmeal Raisin Bread

25 ml/1 fl oz lukewarm water
15 g/½ oz dried yeast
1 tablespoon corn oil
100 g/4 oz rolled oats
1 heaped tablespoon light
   muscovado sugar

2 teaspoons salt
350 g/12 oz wholemeal flour
200 ml/8 fl oz lukewarm milk or
   soya milk
100 g/4 oz raisins

Mix the water and yeast and leave to stand for 20 minutes or until frothy. Pour into a bowl with the oil, oats, sugar, salt and half the flour. Gradually beat in the milk with a wooden spoon. Add sufficient of the remaining flour to make a soft dough.

Turn onto a floured surface and knead until smooth and elastic. This will take about 10 minutes. The dough may be slightly sticky, so add more flour as needed. Place the dough in a greased bowl and cover with a clean cloth. Leave to rise in a warm place for about 1 hour, or until double in size. Punch down and return to the floured surface. Knead in the raisins and shape into a smooth roll. Place in the prepared tin and leave to rise again until double in size – about 40 minutes.

Bake for 1 hour at 180°C/350°F/Gas 4 until the loaf sounds hollow when tapped on the base. Leave on a wire rack to cool.

Rich Cornbread

1 tablespoon dried yeast
100 ml/4 fl oz lukewarm milk
1 egg, beaten
1 tablespoon honey
1½ tablespoons cooking oil

50 g/2 oz fine cornmeal
25 g/1 oz wholewheat flour
2 tablespoons soya flour
½ teaspoon salt

Mix the yeast and milk together and leave to stand for 20 minutes or until frothy. Beat in the egg, honey and oil. Mix the dry ingredients in a bowl. Make a well in the centre and pour in the liquid mixture. Mix well together and turn into an oiled 450 g/1 lb loaf tin. Leave to rise in a warm place for 30 minutes.

Bake at 180°C/350°F/Gas 4 for 40 minutes. Cool and cut into slices to serve.

Spoon Bread

This lovely fluffy 'bread' is served straight from the dish in which it is cooked. It goes well with eggs or with vegetable casseroles.

350 ml/12 fl oz milk
75 g/3 oz maizemeal
50 g/2 oz butter
½ teaspoon salt
1 teaspoon baking powder
4 eggs, separated

Heat all but 1 tablespoon of the milk in the top of a double saucepan, and gradually stir in the maizemeal. Add the butter. Bring the mixture to the boil, stirring all the time, and cook for 10 minutes. Add the salt and cool to lukewarm.

Dissolve the baking powder in the remaining milk and beat with the egg yolks into the cooked mixture. Whisk the egg whites until stiff and fold in. Pour into a buttered casserole and bake at 180°C/350°F/Gas 4 for 45–50 minutes or until well puffed and brown.

Black Bread

This strongly flavoured bread originated in central Europe. It improves with keeping so do not use for at least 2 days after baking.

2 teaspoons dried yeast
1 teaspoon light muscovado
  sugar
300 ml/½ pint lukewarm water
2 tablespoons molasses or black
  treacle
1 tablespoon gravy browning
175 g/6 oz rye flour
25 g/1 oz maizemeal

400 g/14 oz wholemeal flour
1 teaspoon salt
15 g/½ oz firm margarine, cut
  into small pieces
125 g/5 oz potato, cooked and
  sieved
25 g/1 oz bran
½ teaspoon caraway seeds

Mix the yeast, sugar and water and leave in a warm place for 20 minutes or until the mixture is frothy. Stir in the molasses or treacle and gravy browning. Mix together the flours and the salt and rub in the margarine. Stir in the yeast liquid to make a very thick batter. Add the remaining ingredients and mix to a stiff dough. Turn onto a floured surface and knead for about 5 minutes or until the dough is firm and even. Place in a greased bowl and leave to rise in a warm place for 1½ hours.

Knock down the risen dough and knead again. Divide the dough in half and shape into rounds. Place on greased baking trays and leave to rise until doubled in size again. Bake at 180°C/350°F/Gas 4 for 50–60 minutes or until the bread sounds hollow when the base is tapped with the fingers. Leave to cool on a wire rack.

Indian Oatcakes

175 g/6 oz medium oatmeal
50 g/2 oz wholemeal flour
½ teaspoon salt
¼ teaspoon bicarbonate of soda
½ teaspoon ground cumin

½ teaspoon freshly ground black pepper
40 g/1½ oz butter, cut into small pieces
2 tablespoons boiling water

Mix together the oatmeal, flour, salt, soda, cumin and pepper in a bowl. Rub in the butter until the mixture resembles fine breadcrumbs. Use sufficient water to give a soft binding consistency.

Roll out the dough very thinly, between dry greaseproof paper. Cut into rounds using a pudding plate as guide and then cut the rounds into triangles. Place on a greased baking tray and bake at 200°C/400°F/Gas 6 for about 15 minutes or until the oatcakes are crisp. Cool on the tray and serve with butter. Handle with care for they are very fragile.

CHAPTER NINE

Cakes and Biscuits

Peanut Butter Glaze

This makes a delicious soft glaze for any kind of plain cake or buns.

2 tablespoons smooth peanut butter
5 tablespoons milk
175 g/6 oz icing sugar, sifted

Beat the peanut butter and milk to a smooth cream, then gradually beat in the icing sugar. Use at once to ice buns or cakes and leave to stand for 1 hour or so to allow the glaze to set.

If you want to decorate the cake with toasted nuts or other decorations, add these before the glaze sets.

Brazil Nut Cake

225 g/8 oz Brazil nuts, ground
2 eggs, separated
2 tablespoons runny honey
1 tablespoon light muscovado
  sugar

pinch salt
4 tablespoons quark
1 tablespoon lemon juice
2½–3 tablespoons caster sugar

Mix the nuts with the egg yolks, honey and muscovado sugar. Whisk the egg whites with the salt until very stiff. Mix one tablespoonful of the beaten whites into the nut mixture, then carefully fold in the rest of the whites. Spread the mixture into two 15 cm/6 in rounds on a well-oiled baking tray lined with parchment paper. Bake at 180°C/350°F/Gas 4 for about 30–35 minutes. Leave to cool.

Mix the quark with the lemon juice and caster sugar and spread over one layer of the nut cake. Top with the remaining layer of cake. Sprinkle with a little more caster sugar just before serving.

Oatmeal Scones   Makes 12

175 g/6 oz wholemeal flour, sifted to remove some of the bran
50 g/2 oz oatmeal
3 teaspoons baking powder
pinch salt
50 g/2 oz firm margarine, cut into small pieces
50 g/2 oz golden granulated sugar
65 ml/2½ fl oz milk

Place the flour, oatmeal, baking powder and salt in a bowl and mix well together. Rub in the fat until the mixture resembles fine breadcrumbs. Mix in the sugar and sufficient milk to give a light soft dough. Turn the dough onto a floured surface and knead lightly until smooth.

Roll out until the dough is about 2 cm/1 in thick and cut into rounds with a pastry cutter. Place on a lightly floured baking tray and bake at 230°C/450°F/Gas 8 for about 10–12 minutes. Serve warm with butter or cream and jam.

Peanut and Apricot Teabread

*100 g/4 oz firm margarine or
    butter*
50 g/2 oz light muscovado sugar
*100 g/4 oz dried apricots, soaked
    overnight in cold water,
    drained and chopped*

50 g/2 oz ground peanuts
2 eggs
*225 g/8 oz wholemeal flour,
    sifted*
2 teaspoons baking powder
pinch mixed spice

Cream the margarine or butter and sugar until light and fluffy. Add the apricots, peanuts and eggs and beat well. Stir in the flour, baking powder and mixed spice. Spoon into a 450 g/1 lb loaf tin which has been lined with oiled greaseproof paper. Bake at 180°C/350°F/Gas 4 for 35–45 minutes or until lightly browned on top and a skewer inserted into the centre of the teabread comes out clean.

Banana Buckwheat Teabread

*75 g/3 oz butter or firm
    margarine*
*125 g/5 oz light muscovado
    sugar*
2 eggs
3 bananas, sliced

25 g/1 oz raisins
*125 g/5 oz wholemeal flour,
    sifted*
75 g/3 oz ground buckwheat
2 teaspoons baking powder

Cream the butter or margarine and sugar until light and fluffy. Beat in the eggs. Sieve or purée the bananas and add to the mixture with the raisins. Stir in the flour, buckwheat and baking powder. Spoon into a 225 g/8 oz loaf tin which has been lined with oiled greaseproof paper. Bake at 180°C/350°F/Gas 4 for about 1½ hours or until the top is golden brown and a skewer inserted into the centre of the teabread comes out clean.

Coconut Butter Cake

200 g/7 oz self-raising flour
(81% extraction)
200 g/7 oz butter, cut into small
pieces
125 g/5 oz light muscovado
sugar
75 g/3 oz desiccated coconut

1 egg, beaten
4 tablespoons milk
½ teaspoon vanilla essence
milk to glaze

Sift the flour into a bowl. Rub the fat into the flour until the mixture resembles breadcrumbs. Stir in the sugar and coconut. Mix in the egg, milk and vanilla essence to give a tacky dough. Place in a loose-bottomed 20 cm/8 in flan tin and chill for 30 minutes.

Brush with a little more milk and bake at 160°C/325°F/Gas 3 for 30–35 minutes or until well browned. Leave to cool on a wire rack.

Hazelnut Cookies   Makes 10

100 g/4 oz firm margarine or
butter
75 g/3 oz soft brown sugar
(light)
grated rind of 1 orange
150 g/5 oz wholemeal flour

25 g/1 oz ground hazelnuts
1 teaspoon baking powder
10 whole hazelnuts

Cream the margarine or butter and sugar until light and fluffy. Stir in the orange rind. Mix in the flour, ground hazelnuts and baking powder until a firm dough is formed. Break off walnut-sized pieces of dough and shape into balls. Place on a greased baking tray. Flatten each ball a little and press a hazelnut into each one. Bake at 180°C/350°F/Gas 4 for 10–15 minutes or until lightly browned. Leave to cool on the tray for a few minutes, then transfer to a wire rack to cool completely. Store in an airtight container.

Date and Walnut Squares

85 g/3½ oz firm margarine or
   butter
150 g/5 oz wholemeal flour

25 g/1 oz ground walnuts
50 g/2 oz soft brown sugar
   (light)

Filling
100 g/4 oz dates, chopped
25 g/1 oz walnuts, chopped

juice and grated rind of ½ lemon
1 tablespoon honey

Rub the fat into the flour and walnuts until the mixture
resembles breadcrumbs. Add the sugar and knead to form a
smooth dough. Press half the dough into a 14 × 21 cm/5½ ×
8½ in baking tin.

Mix all the filling ingredients together and spread over the
dough in the tin. Press out the remaining dough and place on
top. Bake at 180°C/350°F/Gas 4 for 50 minutes to 1 hour. Cover
with foil halfway through the cooking time. Cool and cut into
squares. Sprinkle with icing sugar if liked just before serving.

Coconut Corn Cake

75 g/3 oz desiccated coconut
6 tablespoons hot water
100 g/4 oz dates, chopped
100 g/4 oz mixed candied peel,
   chopped
150 g/5 oz wholemeal flour
350 g/12 oz yellow cornmeal or
   polenta
2 teaspoons baking powder
¼ teaspoon ground cinnamon

pinch grated nutmeg
pinch ground allspice
100 g/4 oz butter or margarine,
   softened
50 g/2 oz light brown sugar
3 eggs
grated lime rind
120 ml/4 fl oz milk

Mix the coconut and hot water and leave to stand for 30
minutes. Toss the dates and candied fruit in a little of the flour
to keep it separate. Grease a 20 cm/8 in cake tin, sift a little flour
into it and shake round. Sift the rest of the flour into a bowl and

mix in the cornmeal or polenta, baking powder and spices. Cream the butter or margarine and sugar until light and fluffy, then beat in the eggs, one at a time. Beat in half the cornmeal and flour mixture, then add the coconut mixture and milk. Beat in the rest of the cornmeal and flour. Add the candied fruit and dates and a little lime rind and spoon into the prepared cake tin. Bake at 200°C/400°F/Gas 6 for 35–40 minutes or until a skewer inserted in the centre comes out clean. Leave to cool in the tin for 5 minutes, then transfer to a wire rack to cool completely.

Oatmeal Biscuits

Makes 16

These oatmeal biscuits are excellent served with cheese. They are very similar to Scottish oatcakes.

100 g/4 oz oatmeal
75 g/3 oz wholemeal flour
25 g/1 oz sugar
½ teaspoon baking powder

1 teaspoon sea salt
60 g/2½ oz firm margarine or
* butter*
2 tablespoons water

Mix the dry ingredients in a bowl. Cut the margarine or butter into small pieces and rub into the dry ingredients until the mixture resembles fine breadcrumbs. Use sufficient cold water to make a stiff dough. Roll out on a floured board and cut into about 16 rounds using a large pastry cutter. Place on a greased baking tray and bake at 200°C/400°F/Gas 6 for about 15 minutes.

Peanut Fingers

2 tablespoons peanut butter
100 g/4 oz cream cheese
75 g/3 oz dark brown sugar
1 egg
1 tablespoon syrup, honey or
    treacle
½ teaspoon vanilla essence

50 g/2 oz plain flour
¼ teaspoon baking powder
pinch salt
100 g/4 oz rolled oats
75 g/3 oz chopped mixed nuts or
    peanuts

Cream the peanut butter, cream cheese and sugar together. Beat in the egg, syrup and vanilla essence. Add the remaining ingredients and mix to form a thick paste. Press into a 30 × 20 cm/12 × 8 in Swiss roll tin and bake at 180°C/350°F/Gas 4 for 30 minutes or until lightly browned on top. Cut into 14 fingers and leave to cool in the tin for about 20 minutes. Cool completely on a wire rack. Store in an airtight tin.

Millet Flapjacks

Add a little ground ginger or some mixed spice for a change in flavour.

100 g/4 oz butter
50 g/2 oz demerara sugar
1 tablespoon syrup
100 g/4 oz rolled oats
75 g/3 oz millet flakes

Melt the butter in a saucepan. Add the sugar and syrup and mix well together. Stir in the oats and millet flakes. Turn onto a greased baking tray and spread out evenly. Bake at 180°C/350°F/Gas 4 for 30–35 minutes. Cut into bars.

Rye Honey Biscuits   Makes 12

100 g/4 oz rye flour   *½ teaspoon ground cinnamon*
25 g/1 oz light muscovado sugar   *3 tablespoons corn oil*
1 teaspoon bicarbonate of soda   *2 tablespoons runny honey*
1 teaspoon mixed spice

Mix the dry ingredients in a bowl. Add the oil and honey and
mix well together. Shape the mixture into 12 walnut-sized balls
and place on a well-greased baking tray, allowing room for
them to spread. Bake at 220°C/425°F/Gas 7 for 5–6 minutes or
until lightly browned. Leave to cool on the tray for 5 minutes,
then transfer to a wire rack to cool completely.

Cardamom Millet Biscuits   Makes 10

2–3 cardamom pods   *75 g/3 oz butter or firm*
100 g/4 oz millet flakes   *margarine*
75 g/3 oz wholemeal flour   *50 g/2 oz light muscovado sugar*
½ teaspoon baking powder   *1–2 tablespoons water*
½ teaspoon salt

Remove the seeds from the cardamom pods and crush with a
grinder or pestle and mortar. Place in a bowl with the millet
flakes, flour, baking powder and salt. Cut the fat into small
pieces and rub into the dry ingredients until the mixture
resembles fine breadcrumbs. Stir in the sugar and bind with
sufficient water to give a stiff dough. Press out on a floured
board and cut into about 10 biscuits using a pastry cutter. Place
on a greased baking tray and bake at 200°C/400°F/Gas 6 for
20–25 minutes.

Nut Ginger Bread

100 g/4 oz butter or firm
  margarine
100 g/4 oz light muscovado
  sugar
100 g/4 oz treacle or syrup
225 g/8 oz wholemeal flour,
  sifted

50 g/2 oz chopped nuts
1 teaspoon ground ginger
½ teaspoon bicarbonate of soda
pinch salt
1 tablespoon flaked almonds

Cream the fat and sugar together until light and fluffy. Add all
the other ingredients and mix together, beginning with a fork
and ending with your fingers. Do not add any liquid. Press
onto a well-greased or lined 25 × 20 cm/10 × 8 in baking tin.
Bake at 140°C/275°F/Gas 1 for 1 hour and 10 minutes. Cut into
fingers while still hot.

Index